Adoption conversations

what, when and

WITHDRAWN how to tell

Renée Wolfs

Published by
British Association for Adoption & Fostering
(BAAF)
Saffron House
6–10 Kirby Street
London EC1N 8TS
www.baaf.org.uk

Charity registration 275689 (England & Wales) and SC039337 (Scotland)

British Library Cataloguing in Publication Data
A catalogue record for this book is available from the British Library

ISBN 978 1 905664 35 1

Project management by Shaila Shah, BAAF
Photograph on cover posed by models by istockphoto.com
Designed by Andrew Haig & Associates
Typeset by Fravashi Aga
Printed in Great Britain by TJ International Ltd, Padstow, Cornwall
Trade distribution by Turnaround Publisher Services, Unit 3,
Olympia Trading Estate, Coburg Road, London N22 6TZ

BAAF is the leading UK-wide membership organisation for all those concerned
with adoption, fostering and child care issues.

Contents

Acknowledgements

I would like to thank Ansje Bootsma, Fred en Ruke Gundlach, Femmie Juffer, Eva van der Molen, Nelleke Polderman and Liliane Waanders for their dedication and valuable comments on earlier versions. My thanks are also extended to all adoptive parents who, by telephone or email, provided me with examples of conversations with their children. These excerpts (authorised and anonymous) constitute the essence of this guide and demonstate the translation of theory into practice. Finally, I would like to express my love and appreciation to my husband, Marco Borggreve, who ensured that, in spite of our hectic daily schedules, there were always hours in the day for me to write. Without him, this book would not have been completed so quickly.

This book was first written and published in The Netherlands in 2004, under the title *World Child: Talking to your adopted child*. This English language edition has been translated by Jenny van Heyningen and revised by the author.

I would also like to acknowledge the work done by Hedi Argent, Jo Francis and Charis Travlos in editing the English text and preparing the manuscript. My special thanks go to Shaila Shah, for her dedicated work on the English version. Without her, the translated edition would not have been as professional as it is now.

Renée Wolfs
Utrecht, 2008
www.reneewolfs.com

Note about the author

Renée Wolfs is a mother of three children adopted from China. She received her Master's degree in Communication in 1987 and works as a freelance journalist, editor and author. Since 2004, when *World Child* was published in the Netherlands – *Adoption Conversations* is the English language edition – she has written several articles and columns in Dutch adoption magazines.

Her personal involvement in adoption, coupled with her communication expertise and a knowledge of developmental psychology, led Renée to question what exactly children should be told about their adoption story, and at what age. *World Child*, first published in the Netherlands, and now in its fifth edition, was the result. In January 2008, the sequel was published in the Netherlands. Both books have been very well received in the Netherlands and in Belgium. You can find out more on www.reneewolfs.com.

Foreword

The questions come out of the blue: in the bath, in between mouthfuls of cereal, while putting on shoes, with that unmistakeable insistent tone that can't be brushed aside in the bustle of everyday life. 'What happened in China, tell me the whole story again now!', 'Why couldn't my Chinese mother look after me?' or 'Did you love the babies you tried to have more than us?'

Today there is no ducking these questions. In the past, when the subject of a child's adoption came up, it was often hushed away to be explained when they were "old enough to understand" which often meant not until they were grown up. All advice now points to dealing with children's natural curiosity early and as truthfully as possible.

My children were adopted from China and as they grow up they are coming to realise that the way our family was created was rather different from most of their class-mates. Yet all the painful reasons why baby girls are abandoned in China and have been put up for adoption to overseas parents are still too complex and unsettling for them. Instead we try to tell a version of their story so they can absorb it gently. Over the years that story and their understanding of it will evolve.

Finding the best way to discuss our children's roots and the complex process of adoption is important wherever the children are from, whether they are adopted domestically or from overseas. Renée Wolfs focuses in particular on the questions adopted children might ask up to the age of twelve. She takes a down-to-earth approach, calling on her own experience as an adoptive mother as well as a broad sweep of advice from adoption experts and psychologists. This book gives sensible guidelines on how to approach subjects that can be loaded with emotion and anxiety. She suggests ways of wording delicate conversations that can help both children and parents embrace, rather than avoid, some of the thorniest topics. For instance, the book steers the reader through the potential minefield of why birth parents were unable, or not allowed, to look after their child, whether due to social pressure, poverty or abuse.

I am sure *Adoption Conversations* will be a very useful resource for parents whether preparing for the arrival of a child, or to help initiate discussion within the adoptive family.

Emily Buchanan
September 2008

Emily Buchanan is the author of *From China With Love: A long road to motherhood* (John Wiley & Sons, 2005)

Introduction

Adoptive parents today find it very difficult to understand that in past generations many adopted children learned of their adoption only late in life. Yet twenty or thirty years ago, being open about adoption was not the norm, as it is today. Generations of adoptive families could probably write many books about their experiences.

Times have changed for the better. Nowadays, parents are much more aware of the importance of openness. In the past decade, there has been an accumulation of knowledge relating to the significance of adoption for children, birth parents and adoptive parents. With this knowledge, adoption organisations and therapists are better equipped to focus their attention on the specific post-adoption problems of everyone involved. Adoptive families now have many more opportunities to ask for professional support in bringing up their adopted child. There are also a number of specialised courses for adoptive parents, and parent groups where they can meet to share experiences with each other. Additionally, with the arrival of the internet, adoptive parents today can exchange experiences with each other wherever they are, in a hitherto unprecedented way.

As a result of these changing circumstances, a new generation of adoptive parents has developed. A generation of parents who are no longer isolated and required to rely only on their own insights into raising their adopted children. A generation of parents who are now able to pool their experiences and advice with other adoptive parents to help raise their children.

When we adopted our first child, I registered myself with various email discussion groups. Since then, I have exchanged many valuable experiences with other adoptive families. Consequently, I have never felt alone during the responsible, complicated task of raising my young adopted children. The questions we ask each other are often related to openness and to the backgrounds of our children:

> When do I begin to discuss the adoption? At what age is my child ready to hear specific information? Should I tell my child that her birth mother was a drug addict? Is it normal that my child does not want to talk about the adoption? How do I find out what my child is really going through inside? What do I do if my child is angry and says that we are not his real parents? What do I do if my child asks a question that I can't answer directly? How do I handle hurtful comments made by my child's friends or other adults? What do I do if my child says that she did not want to be adopted at all? How do I maintain good communication between myself and my child? Is it normal that my child feels so sad about the adoption? Do all adopted children feel sad? At what stage should I ask for help from an adoption specialist?

Although most parents in the email groups are very willing to be open with their child about his or her background, in practice it seems very difficult to do so, and often, you can be caught by surprise. For example, you're in your car at a busy intersection with your children and suddenly one of them asks: 'Mum, why couldn't my mother care for me?' Or you're in a busy shop and your son says: 'You bought me, Dad, is that right?'

Even with the best of intentions, at that moment you simply don't know what to say. The reason may be that it is not the right time to provide an explanation, or perhaps parents are shocked because the question was so direct and too complicated to discuss at that moment. In other cases, parents are unsure about how much they should tell their child at that specific age, or they feel uncomfortable because the question may be closely related to their own grief about not being able to have birth children of their own.

Although these uncertainties are understandable at these moments, it is nevertheless important that adopted children are able to ask questions at any time and parents should respond in a realistic and open way. Otherwise, there is a chance that the child will feel that his parents are not comfortable talking about adoption and, as a result, instinctively come to the conclusion that questions about his background should not be asked. This could result in the child creating a fantasy world in which he makes up the answers to these questions himself. This fantasising activity can affect the development of the child's own identity in the teen years, with possible difficult consequences.

It is also important that adoptive parents teach their child to talk about their past before they start attending high school. If the child learns at a very early age (between three and seven years old) not to be afraid to talk and share fantasies about her birth parents, culture and the reasons why she was given up for adoption, she will have the best chance to further develop her self-confidence and to put her adoption into perspective.

I searched for information about "openness and communication in adoption" and gathered advice about raising adopted children from some Dutch publications. These books and brochures covered important topics, but none of them focused on communication between parents and their adopted children.

I continued my search on the internet and discovered a number of recent and practical books in the USA about "openness and adoption". Most of these books were written by experienced, leading adoption therapists. I read a lot about the importance of openness and about the complex feelings that adoptive parents and adopted children have. Spread over many pages, I found good advice about how I could react in specific situations. However, I could still not find any adoption literature where the central focus was on "the quality of the communication".

Because I am convinced that communication between parents and their adopted child is of utmost importance, I decided that I would write a book about openness and communication in adoption to supplement the current literature. *Adoption Conversations* is the result, and has become a practical guide in which I have tried to answer the most important questions about adoption that parents may be faced with while raising their child.

While writing this guide, I became even more aware of the complex tasks parents are faced with while raising their adopted children. As adoptive parents, we need to be equipped with more effective ways to communicate with our children about certain issues, in comparison with parents who have birth children.

- We need to be more aware of our patterns of behaviour, and be able to recognise, realise and/or accept our own prejudices and fears. In this way, we have a much smaller chance of transferring our unresolved emotions to our adopted children.
- We have to learn more about the emotional and cognitive development of our children at various stages of life. By doing this, we can relate better to what our children are going through and then reach out to them, understand them and support them during various development stages. We can also better interpret specific questions regarding their adoption and their insecure feelings as a result of being separated from their birth parents.
- We should ideally establish a form of communication that stimulates bonding. For adopted children, this builds more self-confidence, which automatically leads to more openness on the part of the child during conversations.

● We must immerse ourselves in the grieving process that our children experience as a result of their adoption. This offers support for our children during periods when they are feeling anxious, sad or angry about their adoption.

It is easy to treat the theories in this book as "absolute truths". However, this is not my intention. Each child and each parent is different. It is not a given that 'by definition all children of a certain age experience the same problems' or that 'at specific ages, they should be told certain things about their past'. My book is focused on providing practical, communication guidelines; one parent might feel challenged by some of the advice offered, another parent may not. Hopefully, this book will provide insights into adoption topics that you may be faced with periodically and give you tools which you can use to guide your child.

I would also like to emphasise here that I do not wish to stigmatise adopted children in any way. It is true that this book is about the problematic issues you may be faced with while raising your adopted child, but of course it is not the case that you will be dealing with these issues on a daily basis. Adopted children are different, but also belong to the family in a normal way. Although this book covers the differences, it does not imply that adopted children are always "different". What is important is that adopted children receive the message from their parents that they belong to them, but at the same time should be given the space to experience and cope with being "different".

In her book, *Adopted Children: Raising and bonding in the family*, Femmie Juffer (Professor of Adoption Studies at the Center for Child & Family Studies, Leiden University, The Netherlands) writes:

> Adopted children benefit the most from parents who do not reject the difference, but who also do not exaggerate it, but accept it. These parents are giving their children the following message: 'Even with your other past, you belong with us, fully and for good'.

These children can establish themselves in their adoptive family, they can feel at home because the parent does not continuously emphasise their "being different". On the contrary, these parents emphasise the underlying togetherness and belonging. At the same time, the child is given the space to think and to talk about where he comes from, his culture and appearance.
(1999, p. 117)

I hope that you do not read this book with the view that it focuses only on problems. I wrote this book out of love for all adopted children and for all the parents who raise these beautiful children. It is specifically intended to provide you and your child with support during moments of doubt or insecurity. The chapters have been written in such a way that they can also be read independently. Therefore, you can refer to a specific chapter if your child is experiencing a particular issue.

There is a reason for restricting the content of this book to children up to and including 12 years old. By this age, conversations about their adoption should have become common between parents and children. Learning to deal with adopted adolescents and the specific problems relating to adoption that may follow is, to a certain extent, a more complicated task and deserves a book of its own.

For ease of reading and in order not to do injustice to or render invisible either sex, I have chosen to refer to each sex in each alternate chapter.

1

How parents experience adoption

Introduction: preconceived ideas about adoption

Adoption is a complex issue. Many people hold strong opinions about it. Often these opinions stem from stereotypical messages about adoption in the media. They may also be deeply rooted in our cultural background in terms of the ultimate importance of bloodlines and genetic inheritance.

Prospective adoptive parents also often have a clear notion of adoption. It is important to understand why and how this notion has been formed, because unconsciously you might convey these thoughts or feelings to your child. Your feelings about adoption may be influenced by your personal history, or by a range of views from the people in your millieu who, in turn, have also been influenced by opinions that stem from their culture. Only when you understand where your mixed feelings and thoughts about adoption come from can you learn to recognise and deal with them.

In this chapter, I discuss the confusing thoughts and feelings that you may periodically experience about adoption. If you are able to acknowledge, recognise and understand them, you will be more able to separate your feelings from the feelings that your child has about her adoption.

Confusing thoughts and feelings

Should we start the adoption process anyway? People sometimes react quite negatively to our plans.

If people decide to adopt a child, most of them have already come a long way. They may have had to come to terms with their infertility; they may possibly have put aside very strong personal desires to have their "own" child. When you have finally chosen to adopt a child, and you want to share your hopes with the ones you love most, it is not easy when you are confronted with unexpected judgements from family and friends. 'Do you really want to do this?' 'You don't know this child', or 'Do you know what you are getting yourself into?' are common reactions. Some grandparents-in-waiting are disappointed if they don't have a grandchild "of their own". They might blame you for not trying harder to become pregnant. Quite unexpectedly, one of your best friends might raise her eyebrows and wonder 'whether you are aware that adopted children often cause problems'. 'A life without children can also be fulfilling', somebody else might say. Another might carefully ask whether you can 'choose a child whose parents are definitely not alive'.

Such comments could make you feel sad or confused. It is useful to realise that these judgemental attitudes will always exist. People are influenced by books, films and TV programmes about adoption, and by negative reports in the press. Adoption gets everyone's attention; abandoning and being abandoned are ancient themes.

It is often difficult to deal with negative comments from family, friends and acquaintances, but it is important that you learn to cope with them because the reaction of others will intensify once your child is with you. Many opinions expressed by people around you will be based on insufficient factual knowledge and are the result of ignorance. It is in your child's interests and in your interests to combat this ignorance and to deal with it positively as time goes by.

Will I be able to love my adopted child just as much as I would love my birth child?

You may have many doubts while you prepare for adoption. Your feelings might stem from the intense wish you still have, or have had, for a birth child. Or you may already have a birth child whom you love very much. Your feelings could also be influenced by deep-rooted cultural beliefs about the importance of "blood ties". In some cultures it is difficult to understand that parents can love other people's children or that a "real" parent–child relationship can exist if the mother does not give birth to the child in question. But a good bond between adults and children develops mostly as a result of lasting, loving and everyday care, and not only because a child is genetically related to the parent. Your child may be unlike you, but this does not mean that there will be less of a bond with her.

You may wonder whether you will love this "stranger" as soon as she arrives. This is very understandable: the initial period is often not the magical, "rosy" time that parents have when their first child is born. Although parents who have birth children also need to get used to their child and the bonding process sometimes takes a little longer than expected, adoptive parents have a more complicated task. In most cases, the mutual bonding process with adopted children takes a long time, sometimes even several years. Your child may have behavioural problems, she may often ignore you or she may cling to you day and night. During these times, you might doubt whether it is actually true that you can love adopted children as much as if they had been born to you. An adoptive mother writes:

> The first two years with our daughter were very difficult. Mischa was grieving. She was unsettled, sad,

anxious and continually sought conflicts...We decided to attend an adoption course. I thought that it was important to be open about our uncertainty and to ask for support when we needed it. It was an enormous relief when somebody during this course said: 'You and your child don't need to love each other immediately. You have both experienced so much. First work out how both of you can get through this stage.' And that gave me some breathing space.

(From *Adoptietijdschrift no.2*, jrg 6, June 2003)

As your adopted child gets older, more doubts may surface about "how real and how deep" the love is that you feel for your child, especially if she periodically distances herself from you or behaves destructively. It is important to realise that these feelings of uncertainty are common to many families, not only adoptive ones. A lot of parents have a preference for a particular child in a family and experience another child as "more difficult". This does not mean that you love the other child any less, it merely means that you get on better with the one than with the other. If you accept the differences, you will most probably form a closer bond with all your children.

If we had children of our own, they would look more like us and we would probably be able to understand each other better.

Even if you have come to terms with your childlessness and you love your adopted child very much, there can be moments when you have difficulty with the differences between you and your child. You may possibly be disappointed that your child doesn't physically resemble you in any way. You may also have some problems with the fact that you and your child have different temperaments, or a significantly different level of intelligence. Maybe you have a friend whose children achieve better results at school or who have the same interests and talents as their parents, and this serves to further emphasise the differences between you and your child.

It is understandable that you sometimes wonder what it would have been like to have a child who was genetically yours. Most parents who have adopted a child, for whatever reason, do sometimes have these thoughts. It is best to simply accept these feelings. By doing so, you will avoid developing feelings of guilt that you may then transfer to your child. Femmie Juffer comments:

> It is good if parents and therapists understand that dealing with involuntary childlessness is a life-long process that does not automatically end once you have adopted a child. I am possibly over-emphasising this, but to ensure that it is well understood, I want to add that I don't think that it is because of unacknowledged childlessness that adoptive parents from time to time realise that it would have been different if they had had birth children. On the contrary, I think that especially parents who recognise the differences and who are willing to think and talk about it, have acknowledged and accepted their childlessness. (1999, pp. 120–121)

In genetically related families, parents may also wonder what it would have been like if they had had a different child. Couples often think that they will produce children who will resemble them but, in reality, there are no guarantees. Just as children sometimes fantasise about having other parents, parents also fantasise about having other children.

I wanted us to be a "normal family". Everyone interferes with us and when we are in public we are never anonymous.

Often from the moment adoptive families bring their child home, they are confronted with unwelcome attention. Comments often confirm the prejudice people have about adoption, sometimes in a subtle, but sometimes in a very direct way. 'She looks a little like you, did you know that?' is one of the more subtle, well-intentioned comments that are made by friends or strangers. As if that made the family look "normal"! Or 'Aah, what sweethearts! Are they sisters?' As if the blood link resulted in "stronger sisterhood"! Or someone points at the buggy, laughs affectionately and says: 'What a cutie, where does he come from?' Or 'Is he yours?', 'What a pity they all start searching for their real parents later on in life,' and 'Oh, what a tiny little girl! She should be very grateful!' These comments can be made by total strangers, with good intentions, but they highlight the prejudice and misunderstandings that exist about adoption. The parents and child get the feeling that they are special in a certain way, but also that everyone has an opinion about them. Personal questions can sometimes be asked while mother and child are out together, for example, while queuing at the post office: 'Couldn't you have children of your own?', or, if your child has a visible disability, 'Oh, what a shame. Couldn't you choose another one?'

You may respond with anger or be dismissive; you will want to protect your child from insensitive family and friends or ignorant strangers. No matter how understandable your reaction is, it is nevertheless important that you realise what is being conveyed to your child. If you frequently feel insecure or affected by unhelpful comments, your child will feel the same, no matter how hard you try to conceal it. She may then receive a negative impression of her adoption.

It is better to try to keep your own feelings insulated from societal prejudices, however difficult that may be; these prejudices exist and you can only try to change them in your own social network. Hurtful comments made by strangers often reflect general attitudes and are not particularly directed at you, your adopted child or your family. If you understand and accept this, you will probably be able to deal with inappropriate comments a lot more positively, and you can show and teach your child that people do not ask questions because they want to be malicious, but out of ignorance. Your child can then feel good about her adoption, which will help to develop trust, and eventually enable her to cope in today's society.

An adoptive family is always "special". It is a fact that you can't or shouldn't fight against. During the entire process of raising your child, you will be confronted with different advice and opinions, some good and some bad.

My child would have been much happier if she could have grown up in her own environment. We shouldn't have adopted her.

When adopted children go to school, they may be directly confronted with the fact that they are different. Classmates who are not yet six years old will say, in their childlike, direct way: 'Did they throw you away?' or 'You have a stupid name'. Your child might be mocked about her looks or teased because she doesn't have a "real" mother.

As a result, your child might sometimes ask you how it all happened. She might sigh a lot and say: 'I don't want to be adopted', or 'I want different eyes', or 'Why didn't you leave me in Colombia?'

At such moments, you may question your conscience: 'Did we do the right thing by taking this child out of her own environment? Why did we so urgently have to fulfill our wish for a child? She is sad and longs for her native country and her "first" mother. She wants to share her sadness and insecurity with us, but are we able to help her? Is our happiness not due to her sadness and that of her birth parents?'

It is logical to have these doubts. For hundreds of years, many experts have been questioning whether adoption is the best alternative for a child who is, or needs to be, separated from their birth parents. Every child has the right to grow up in her own culture, speak her own language and to have her own family. However, sometimes the choice to adopt is justified because otherwise the child would not have the opportunity to grow up in a loving family. Your child was given up for adoption for this reason. If you hadn't adopted this child, she would have been adopted by another family. The fact that she is adopted is a completely separate matter from your wish to have a child. She will feel sad about her adoption during certain periods in her life, no matter who adopted her. You will support your child by putting your feelings of guilt and doubts aside and by teaching her to cope with being different.

Can I actually raise a child? Will I do a good job? I might not be a good mother. I owe the other mother a lot.

These questions, which you may have had prior to the adoption, may resurface when your child actually arrives. On the one hand, you might be overwhelmed by feelings of joy, but on the other hand, it might bother you that your happiness comes at the cost of the sadness of the birth parents. One adoptive mother writes movingly about the arrival of her three-month-old son:

> It feels like it happened yesterday. I could not believe it was finally true; the waiting was over. Only two weeks later I held my little boy, Dion, for the first time in my arms. He was a very small boy with dark hair and very big eyes, and he looked up at me curiously. A wonderful moment, a wonderful son. However, I didn't immediately feel like "his mother". There was a mother somewhere in Colombia who gave birth to Dion. For that, I owe this unknown woman very much. She has trusted me with her son. All these thoughts made me feel insecure. In the beginning, I did not allow myself to make mistakes. It all had to go well. Luckily, it did. (From *Adoptietijdschrift* no.3 (2002), 'Het leek allemaal zo simpel...', Drieluik 'de adoptie-ouder')

Another adoptive mother writes about her feelings of guilt:

> After the arrival of my first child, it was difficult to cope
> with the enormous feelings of responsibility. Can I
> actually raise a child and will I do it well? It was like the
> birth mother was looking over my shoulder all the time.
> It was very difficult to give the birth mother a place in
> my heart. I felt that I had taken her child away from
> her, that I was building my happiness around her
> sadness. If my daughter giggled at me or if I proudly
> strolled through the town with her, I felt a deep sadness
> for her mother who would not be able to experience
> any of this. But after a while, I realised also that her
> mother gave her up for adoption in order to give her
> the chance of having a happy childhood. I understood
> that nobody would benefit from my feelings of guilt.
> (From *Adoptietijdschrift* no.3 (2002), 'Het leek allemaal
> zo simpel...', Drieluik 'de adoptie-ouder')

If you are in doubt about your right to motherhood or fatherhood,
you may be influenced by the fact that you couldn't have children
of your own. Parents sometimes experience their childlessness as a
"judgement", a sign that they are not suitable to be parents and to
raise a child. Women who have had miscarriages also sometimes
feel that they have "failed as a woman". You must realise that these
feelings have no basis. People who are involuntarily childless have
had bad luck, just like people with a disability or a disease. That's
the way it is, and you can do nothing about it. In spite of your
childlessness and the sadness and despair you have endured, you
have decided to give a child in need a better chance in life. You are
open to new experiences and that is one of the qualities that will
probably make you good parents.

The fact that you cannot have children of your own and that you
chose to adopt a child has nothing to do with your abilities to raise
a child. It is important to realise this, otherwise you might develop
an idealist image of the birth mother as fertile, possibly very

beautiful, young and longing for her child. Eventually, this fantasy can become so appealing that you start believing that the birth mother is a rival. If the birth parents begin to be a threat to you, your child will feel this and will no longer want to, or dare to, talk about them.

You should also realise that no parent is perfect. All parents make mistakes and often feel that they should do better. That does not mean that other parents are nicer or do a better job.

I can't handle the fact that my child was abandoned/mistreated. I can't understand how her parents/carers could have done this to her. I find it very difficult to say nice things about them.

Maybe you don't have an ideal image of the birth parents, but predominantly feel anger towards them, perhaps because you regularly see your child struggling with the consequences of their actions. You know that under no circumstances would you have abandoned your birth child. The reasons for your anger might also stem from your adopted child's painful past; she may have been abused or seriously neglected. An adoptive father writes about his distress and anger at what had happened to their children before they had come to them:

> Our eldest daughter was abandoned when she was two months old. We adopted her when she was about one year old. Four years later we adopted her brother, who was then two-and-a-half years old. He was abandoned in the street when he was two. He had scars on his arms and legs but no one knew how they originated. We also knew nothing about his past. Last month, my daughter, who is seven years old now, asked: 'Dad, could I walk when they found me?' I shook my head and said: 'You were a little baby and they wrapped you in a warm blanket and put you at the entrance to a school where

somebody would find you very quickly'.

She had asked these questions before, but this time a question about her brother followed: 'Could Boaz walk when they found him?' 'Yes', I said, 'Boaz was two years old and could walk very well.' She went silent and after a few minutes she carried on: 'That must have been very scary for him because he had to cross the road all by himself.' I got all choked up and I felt such anger and sadness. Sadness for my son who, at this moment, isn't aware of what happened to him but will, in the near future, realise that he was a toddler who was left completely alone. At the same time, I was so furious at what his birth parents had done to him. He was with them for two years. What parents abandon their child after two years? He has scars and not a day goes by that we don't ask ourselves how they got there. Did his parents abuse him? Was he tied to his bed at the orphanage? I find it very difficult to think in a positive way about his parents or the orphanage he came from.

It is important to realise that your child will not benefit from your anger. Adopted children often develop better if they are able to accept their past and if they can identify with their birth parents in a positive way, no matter how little good there is to identify with. Her birth parents gave life to her and she is genetically 100 per cent their child. If her parents were "bad", she could conclude that she is also "bad" and that she has no right to exist. Don't let her notice your angry feelings towards her birth parents, even if she herself expresses negative thoughts about them.

You and your partner might each think differently about the birth parents; you might also each feel differently about the loyalty you feel towards them. However, as far as your child is concerned, it is best not to reveal any conflicting feelings but, instead, to try and express the same feelings about the birth parents to your child, so that she does not become even more confused.

I cannot confront my child with the sadness that we have endured about our childlessness.

For many parents, the sadness of their infertility is a difficult subject, especially when their child wants to know more about it. Questions from young adopted children like 'Why am I living with you?' or 'Why was I not in your tummy, Mummy?' sometimes affect parents deeply. A mother of a seven-year-old daughter recalls her difficulty in talking about this:

> I remember clearly when my daughter asked us why we didn't have children of our own. Up until then we had been very open about her adoption, we were able to keep it simple and positive, but suddenly there was this difficult moment. I hesitated and felt uncertain. I responded in an unclear manner and changed the subject very quickly. Later, when I had time to think it over, I understood why I felt so uneasy. I had to tell her we couldn't have children of our own and that was the reason she was with us. I was afraid to tell her that we wanted to have our own children. I did not want her to feel that she was second best because I love her so much.

> My daughter is two years older now, and we regularly and openly discuss this subject. Naturally, I am sad about the fact that we could not have our own children, but that does not mean that I don't love my daughter very much. I cannot imagine my life without her. If I could do everything over again and become pregnant, I would prefer to have her in my womb. I share these feelings with her. I will, however, never forget how difficult it was the first time I had to talk about my infertility. I love my child so much, how could I ever tell her that she would not be here if I could have had children of my own? Sometimes, I still find it difficult to think about it.

It is important to realise that infertility will always be a factor in your life, although for some this feeling will be stronger than for others. Your uncertainty and sadness in this regard are probably just as strong as your child's hesitation and sadness about her adoption. Show your child that you felt sad or maybe still feel sad. You can support each other because your child also knows what sadness is. She would also have liked to have been your "own" child, which means: she would prefer not to be adopted. The fact that you have found a way to be happy despite your sadness may help your child to deal with her own sadness too.

I can't be strict with my child. She has been through so much already.

As a result of your child's painful past, you may feel sorry for her and therefore you may find it difficult to be strict with her, as this adoptive mother writes:

> In the first few months, I couldn't believe that Tanya was actually with us. We had waited for her for so long. When we adopted her, she looked very neglected – she was just two-and-a-half years old but she had to roam the streets and nobody had really looked after her. Now, she has been with us for two years. She is very naughty. I find it difficult to be strict with her. When she does something that is not allowed, I want to correct her but she often reacts with fear if I get angry with her. I prefer to just let her do what she likes, even if she is naughty. I will never forget how neglected and lonely she looked when we adopted her. She has already been through so much.

Your child has the best chance of building basic trust if you raise her in a consistent and structured environment. It doesn't matter how sad you feel when you think about her past – she will not benefit from your pity. You can be firm without being angry or having to raise your voice. It is also important to choose your words well and to be consistent when making decisions and agreements with your child. In Chapter 5, I discuss how parents can be strict without getting angry.

My child is still so young. I want to spare her from the pain of her adoption history for as long as possible. I want her just to be a child and to participate at school in a normal way.

It is natural that parents want to protect their children from sadness for as long as possible. Babies and young children are, around the world, a symbol of purity and innocence. Adopted children often lose this innocence at an early age and this is very difficult for parents to accept; they want to protect their adopted children from pain.

Maybe you feel hopeless knowing that you have to tell your child all about her sad past. An adoptive father who has an eight-year-old son writes:

> I find it unbearable to notice that his adoption background causes him so much pain. It also hurts me terribly. I find it incredibly difficult and would like to take the pain away from him.

It might sound contradictory to say that your child will benefit most if you tell the story as early as possible, but if you talk openly with your child about the adoption from the beginning and you share the sadness together, then your child will probably establish trust in you, feel safe and become emotionally strong. Even if your child does not ask about it, it is important that you tell her about her past as soon as possible. It is also very important that you explain things at a level that she can understand, depending on her age and abilities, at the time (see Chapters 2 and 3).

Many people think that if you don't stir up the reasons for the sadness, then the sadness will be reduced. Actually, the opposite is true. If you don't allow the tears to flow, they build up. At a certain point, "the bucket will overflow". And it may overflow with great intensity.

Children who experience adoption-related grief most probably have the same reason as you do for suppressing it: they are afraid of the deep emotions that make them feel vulnerable. If these children are able to express these feelings, they are letting you know that they feel safe with you. At such moments, it is very important that you always validate your child's feelings and don't try to avoid the subject.

Question yourself as to why you are afraid of your child's adoption-related grief. You may, yourself, not have come to terms with an experience of loss. Most adults have experienced the loss of someone or something special in their lifetime. If you did not allow your emotions to be expressed and acknowledged, then this may have an impact on how you face your child's loss. In the course of their lifetime, adopted children grieve periodically for their birth parents to a lesser or greater degree. If you are scared of grief, you can unconsciously or unintentionally transfer this fear to your child; her grieving process can thereby be inhibited. Chapters 8 and 9 discuss in more detail the adoption-related grief that your child will experience, and also deal with the question of how you can handle it in the best way.

Our child will probably leave us later, as she will want to return to her native country/find her birth parents.

If you feel insecure about being adoptive parents, you may easily think that your child might leave you sometime in the future to be with her "real" parents. This feeling is totally understandable, especially if your child periodically rejects you. Cultural perceptions about the importance of a blood relationship can confirm a fear of abandonment, as can documentaries or movies which focus on finding and bringing together adopted children and their birth families.

If abandonment is an issue for you that raises many complex emotions, then you might convey these to your child. Adopted children are themselves often troubled by the fear of being abandoned again. Your child will benefit most from a well-considered appreciation of her personal fear brought about by her adoption.

Conclusion

As I said at the beginning of this chapter, adoption is a complex matter. It is consciously and unconsciously affected by other people's reactions, by cultural perceptions and by the personal life history of all involved. It is important that you are aware of your own conscious and unconscious feelings that you have developed over time, so that you can think about them more objectively and talk about them more realistically. No matter how difficult it is, try to separate your own emotions and opinions from those of your child; she also has feelings about her adoption and her birth parents and she wants to be able to talk openly to you about them.

In the following chapter, I discuss adoption from the child's point of view. If you have insights into your own and your child's inner world, you will probably be more able to understand your child, and to guide her through her adoption history.

2

How children experience adoption

Being in tune with your child's stage of development

Adoptive parents often wrongly interpret comments made or questions asked by their adopted children about their past. I remember so well how emotional I felt when I told my eldest child that another mother gave birth to her. After the first sentence I had to stop to breathe; however, my two-and-a-half-year-old daughter looked at me laconically and a minute later, carried on playing as if nothing had been said. At her age, she felt no sadness as a result of the separation from her birth parents. Even children between three and five years old may not yet be aware of their loss. They live here, with this mother and father, and that is enough. They register what you have said, but only as they grow older will their curiosity grow and will they start asking questions.

With slightly older children, parents sometimes misjudge their child's level of understanding. Children of five or six years of age, for example, do not yet really understand the concept of a genetically related family. They are also not yet capable of relating to other people's experiences and this means that their fantasies about their

birth mother are much less emotional than adopters often think
they are.

Only by the time children are seven or eight do they start to realise
what it really means to be adopted; only at this point will they
realise that they were abandoned when they were young. This is
why adopted children between the ages of seven and 12 often feel
emotional and start grieving. Because of their intense emotions,
they may resist talking about their adoption and their past, for long
periods. Parents may think they should respect this "silent" time.
Their child now knows (broadly) what it all means. However, during
this period, your child may need your understanding even more than
before, but in a different way.

In this chapter, the various developmental phases of children up to
13 years old are discussed. It is important to know that these age
categories are approximate. Despite their age, children vary in terms
of how "developed" they are; this is not linked to their level of
intelligence. Development can be one or two years, sometimes even
three or four years, ahead or behind. In the following section I refer
to average ages because most children (approximately) fall into
these categories.

Babies and toddlers: 0–3-year-olds

Level of understanding

Babies and toddlers don't understand anything about adoption. This
gives you the chance to familiarise your child with a fundamental
and well-chosen adoption vocabulary where you, for example, talk
about "birth mother" instead of "real mother". In this way, your
toddler will become accustomed to a number of words relating to
adoption which he can, at a later stage, question you about. By
discussing adoption from such an early age, the facts are never new,
and your child will always have known that he was adopted in the
same way as he has always known that he was a boy or a girl. You

can also talk about his birth country in a positive way and about the exciting journey to his new country. In this way your child will learn on a basic level that he "belongs to this family through adoption"; in other words, that he "came from another country far away" and that he was "brought home on a plane".

Emotional development

Babies and toddlers do not consciously realise that they are being abandoned by their birth parents. Very young children can, however, instinctively feel sad or fearful as a result of the actual separation. Babies and toddlers must build up basic trust through a healthy attachment to their primary carers. If this essential attachment process is interrupted by an abrupt separation from their trusted carers and environment, they can develop physical symptoms or react by inconsolable crying or angry behaviour. They are given new parents who have strange (and therefore often frightening) habits, who speak another language and who live in a cold country with unfamiliar smells. For children who are approximately between one and two years old, this transition can be especially difficult. They are already aware of their environment, but their understanding of the language is still inadequate. They see but don't understand what has happened and this can make them feel very confused and insecure.

Babies and toddlers can feel safer in these early days if they have a predictable, structured daily routine without too many new experiences. It is best to restrict the number of adult carers, especially during the first months. Some babies and toddlers may be bad tempered, cry a lot, feel anxious at night or have nightmares. Others may remain very quiet or withdrawn, focus their attention on strangers instead of on their new parents, or they may cling to their new mother or father and not let them out of their sight.

Only when children notice that their new caretakers are consistently responding to their emotional and physical needs will they begin to feel safer and relax. During this first phase, you should try never to get angry with your child – it will serve no purpose. Stay calm, tell your child his behaviour is not acceptable and provide him with an alternative (see Chapter 5). Setting boundaries is useful, and reasonable rules will also enhance basic trust and attachment, but becoming angry is not an option. One child will react fearfully and will do everything that is expected of him; another will distance himself from his parents with whom he still does not have a safe bond, and will have no interest in listening to them. In both cases, becoming angry will not create a healthy attachment.

It is important to realise that adopted children need a period of a few weeks or months to get used to their new environment. How long this takes will depend on your child. During this period, the focus must be on helping your child to get used to the new situation. Some children will have problems sleeping or eating; others will not dare to make eye contact or will object every time their parents pick them up. Children need to be given the space to overcome their basic fears and problems.

Once children are used to their new environment, it is time to create opportunities for intimate physical contact. If possible, carry your child in a baby carrier. If your child enjoys sleeping in your bed, consider letting him sleep with you at night. Carry your baby as much as you can, possibly with his face turned away from you until he is quite used to you. You can build up physical contact in a number of ways, and in ways which feel comfortable and safe to the child: at bath time; by gently massaging him before or after sleeping; by putting him on your lap and reading a book or listening to music together. It is also important, during this phase, to express in words his sad or angry behaviour without disapproving of it (see also Chapter 5). If your child cries, say that you know he is sad and in the meantime hold him lovingly. Do not try to suppress this sadness; he may get the feeling that he is not allowed to be sad, or that he can only feel sad to a certain extent. While playing, or during the daily routine, you can name your child's behaviour by describing what he has done or made:

You built a tower.

You ate everything up.

If you continuously confirm what he does or what he feels, he learns that he is being "seen and understood" by you.

It can also be very effective to play "peekaboo" games with your very young child in the early days, so that he will learn that you are always there, even if he can't see you. For example, when your child goes to bed, you could play a game by disappearing behind the door or bed. You can back up this game by repeatedly saying that you are still there, even when you close his door at night, and that you will always stay with him.

The technique of reacting in a sensitive and responsive way by "acknowledging" is discussed in Chapter 5. Chapters 8 and 9 go into the grieving process in more detail. In those chapters, you will also find advice about getting used to and bonding with toddlers and young children.

Young children: 3–7-year-olds

Level of understanding

In this age group, there are two distinct stages: age 3–5 and age 5–7. During the first stage, physical development plays the dominant role. During the second stage, the brain matures rapidly and the child develops a greater intellectual capacity. The level of understanding and emotional development are closely linked at this age. A young child can feel an emotion which is caused by a concept that he is not yet able to fully comprehend, or that he interprets wrongly.

An understanding of adoption begins to develop at this age, but it has not yet fully crystallised. It is very important that you tell your child about his adoption often, and in a clear, simple manner and that you are alert to the fact that he might misinterpret what you have said. It is during this period that children begin to fantasise and to fill in the gaps themselves, which may have disturbing consequences (see below).

Emotional development

Children at this age are often still very self-centred. Their social development progresses only minimally. Although it looks like they are enjoying playing with their friends, these friendships are not yet real friendships. Most children simply notice that it is far more fun playing with somebody else than it is to play alone. If your child shows a preference for one or two children, this is mainly because he knows these children well if he plays with them regularly.

As a result of this self-centredness and because their understanding of reality is still restricted, a child of this age can develop fears that are not always fully detected by an adult, for example, a child may be scared of the idea that he was "in another woman's tummy". A story that was previously nice and exciting and that he wanted to hear often has turned into a story that may no longer be told. In this phase, your child may also blame himself for being given up for adoption by his birth mother. In his self-centred world, he thinks that he is the cause of sadness, death or loss.

Most children between the ages of three and five have a fear of being separated; when your child goes to junior school for the first time, he might doubt whether you will actually come back to collect him. Adopted children especially, who were effectively deserted, can be affected by this intense feeling again in a new, comparable situation. Some children may even feel that they have been "sent away" by their adoptive parents during their first term at school.

Children who are between the ages of five and seven can find it difficult to be "different" at school. From about the age of six or seven, they would prefer to be the same as everyone else and that means they do not want to have brown skin, a strange name or Asian eyes. At this age, children differentiate themselves from others by physical features. If a child of five or six is asked who he is, he will answer: 'I am Josh and I have brown eyes. I look like my father and next week it's my birthday and I am getting a new bike.' It can be very frustrating for children under eight if they can't say that they look like their father or mother. They also 'don't want to be adopted', they would prefer to 'have come out of my own mum's tummy, just like everyone else in the class', and they don't want to be singled out as a result of their adoption. Adopted children are sometimes teased about being different, just as all "different" children are teased about not fitting in with the norm. But children don't always talk to their parents about being teased (see Chapter 7). At this stage, it is better not to emphasise the adoption too much; at the same time, it is important to keep your finger on the pulse as, if you watch carefully, your child might want to talk about uncomfortable moments with friends at school. It is best to let him know that differences among people can be very fascinating.

If you are keeping up with this emotional development, you won't be surprised that your child doesn't always come home with things that you would like to know. However, adopted children are sometimes confronted with difficult comments or questions to which they respond by behaving in an odd or withdrawn way. It is important that you pay attention to any changes in your child's behaviour. If you can't reach him by talking to him, you can try reaching him through play. It is also important to create one-to-one moments while washing the dishes, during a walk or a ride in the car or before he goes to sleep. By doing this, your child will have the chance to ask any questions, and you will be able to determine his real feelings.

Misinterpretations and fantasies

Adopted children probably fantasise about their birth mother at this age. Questions about their birth father are rarely asked until children understand that not only a mother is required for a baby, but also a father. Below are listed a number of confusing thoughts that children can have about their adoption and their birth parents.

You are not my real mother.

There can be confusion about the term "real mother" if children at school learn from their friends that a "real mother" is the one who gave birth to them. Many adopted children are told by their peers that their mother is not their "real mother". It is important that you are prepared for this situation and that you clear up the misunderstanding in advance. You can explain that some children are part of a family through birth and others through adoption, but that both families are "real". From age six or seven, you can also explain that 'all dads and mums have filled in official papers and that a judge has said that they are the real forever-mum-and-dad' (see Chapter 7).

My birth mother will come and adopt me back one day.

These thoughts can occur if your child has not yet fully grasped the meaning of the adoption process. He doesn't understand that the adoption is final and he may wonder whether the adoption can be reversed: if his birth mother decided that she couldn't take care of him, could she one day decide that she wants to look after him again?

Children at this age need constant reassurance about their adoptive status so that they understand that they won't be taken away by their birth parents, and that their adoptive parents are their "real parents".

If my adoptive parents didn't adopt me, I would still be with my birth mother.

Your child doesn't yet fully understand the reasons for adoption, therefore he may fill in some gaps for himself. He may blame you for knowingly taking him away from his birth parents. He may then behave in a way that you don't understand: he could get into a rage or even be aggressive or out of control, he could become hyperactive, or just very quiet and anxious. You could possibly avoid some of this by going over and over the adoption process at this stage. However, these kinds of misinterpretations aren't totally avoidable. In this specific case, you can be clear about the fact that you did not take him away, but that his birth parents decided to give him up for adoption. He would therefore, in any case, have been adopted, even if you hadn't become his parents.

My adoptive parents left me at the orphanage for two years before they adopted me.

These thoughts also stem from the fact that the adoption process is not fully understood. From about age five or six, it is good to regularly explain that birth parents and the social worker and judges want to be sure that children get a good mother and father, and that takes time. Adopters have to see a lot of people and fill in a lot of official papers before they are allowed to become parents. You could also tell your child that if he had been adopted by other parents, he would also have had to wait two years.

It is my fault that my mother gave me up for adoption.

These thoughts exist because young children "think magically": they believe that they are at the centre of the world and therefore they make everything happen. Many children think that difficult, painful or sad situations are their fault. Adopted children often feel guilty, just as children feel guilty after a divorce or after the death of a pet or a special member of the family. Adopted children may feel that they weren't nice, healthy or beautiful enough or that they are the wrong sex and that was why they were given up for adoption. They may get the idea that they always have to be nice because otherwise they will be given away once again. It is important to reassure your child that he was not given up for adoption because

he wasn't nice or beautiful, or any other wrongly perceived
characteristic. From about the age of seven, you can explain that he
was not rejected as a person, but that his birth parents couldn't look
after a baby – any baby.

I was abandoned in the street and then I had to cry very loudly and I was totally alone for a long time.

Adopted children of this age know that they were "born and
abandoned" and that after a while they were "adopted". However,
they sometimes know nothing or very little about the period
between being abandoned and the adoption. By fantasising about
this period they can develop fears: 'What if my new parents
wouldn't have been there to adopt me? Would I still be without
parents? Would I have died? How long was I lying in the street?
Was it cold and dark? Did I have to cry a lot and did people actually
hear me?' It can be frightening for your child to know that he was
lonely, staying with strange children and strange carers. It is
important that you are aware of fantasies like these during this
phase of development.

You could tell your child how he was abandoned; that he wasn't
cold, lonely and alone in the street, but, for example, that he was
put down in a place where there were many people so that he
would be found very quickly. If your child was brought to the
authorities by a family member, or if he was immediately handed
over to them after being born, it is also important to explain the
steps that followed. Try to tell him about it in a positive way, but do
not make it sound too nice, because when your child is older he will
find out if you did not tell the truth, and this would damage the
trust between you and your child.

If you don't know anything about the period between your child
being abandoned and being adopted, it is better to tell your child
that you know nothing about that time. But you could add that,
despite the adoption, your child's birth parents most probably loved
him. You could say: 'Your birth mother wouldn't have left you with

very few clothes. I am almost sure you were dressed warmly.'

I was not born, I was adopted.

It is still very difficult for young children to distinguish between the story of their birth and the story of their adoption. A girl who was talking to her adopted friend about the birth of her brother, asked: 'When were you born?' The adopted boy replied: 'I was not born, I was adopted.' These thoughts can exist if you put too much of a celebratory emphasis on the day of the adoption and if you forget to talk about the special moment when your child was born (even if you do not know the precise date of birth). It is vital that your child feels he has been welcomed into your family from the beginning, but it is just as important that he learns that he was just as welcome when he was born. Ultimately, he needs to be able to identify with both families.

Confusion can also occur about conception. This is what a five-year-old asked her mother: 'Mum, did Dad give his seed before I was adopted or after?' This question is quite normal for a five-year-old and requires a good answer!

My adoptive parents love me, therefore one day they can also decide to give me up.

Young children, but also older children up to the age of 12, may develop this fear. You most probably talk about the birth parents in a loving way. This is necessary for your child's sense of identity, but you need to be aware that this positive and open approach may cause some uncertainty. Be careful how you phrase it and, for example, don't say: 'Your mother loved you so much that she chose the best for you; that is why she gave you up for adoption.' Some children will start thinking that if you love them, you may also give them up for adoption. You could say instead: 'Your birth mother could not take care of you at that moment in her life, but she did want the best for you and that is why she gave you up for adoption.'

If my parents are very angry with me, they can send me away.

Children often think that when parents are very angry with them, they don't love them. Adopted children have been abandoned once before. More than other children, they need confirmation that you love them unconditionally, even if you are angry. Always make it clear to your child that being angry does not mean that you don't love him. Explain to him that you are angry because of his behaviour at that moment. You could say to your toddler or young child: 'I love you very much, but I don't love it when you scream.'

It sounds paradoxical but it is often precisely the children who have already been rejected or abandoned once who push the boundaries to see if it will happen again. Children who are scared of being left will continually test their parents' reliability. This is why adopted children often display quite extreme behaviour. If they are angry they sometimes mean the opposite: 'Please don't leave me, stay with me forever, hold me tight!' By being angry or behaving aggressively, they are trying to test their parent's love. During puberty, this behaviour may become even more extreme.

Frequently asked questions

From approximately two years:

- Where do children come from?
- Where do I come from?
- Was I in your tummy?
- Were my sisters/brothers in your tummy?
- Why didn't you have any children in your tummy?

From approximately five years:

- Why couldn't my mother look after me any longer?
- Why did you take me with you?
- How did I get here?
- Can my mother come and take me back?

It is important during this phase to encourage questions and to answer them simply and factually. If you try hard to listen to your child and watch him when he plays, when he talks to friends, or draws and paints, you can usually find out whether he has a realistic understanding of adoption.

Children in primary school: 7–12-year-olds

Level of understanding

When children reach junior school level, they become more independent and need less intensive guidance. Nevertheless, this is a "difficult age". Because your child is more active outside the home, you spend less time with him. It may seem like he is too busy to bother about his adoption, but many thoughts may trouble him during these years.

At this age your child develops the ability to think abstractly. From about eight years old he is also able to put himself in somebody else's shoes. He learns to understand that families are mostly formed through a genetic relationship and he will probably begin to ask himself: If families are formed by a blood relationship, then which family is my "real" family? Who is my birth mother and what does she look like? Are she and my father doing well? Do I look like them? Is everything alright? Are they sick or unhappy?

Because children at this age understand the full meaning of adoption, they will also realise that they were "given away". Most adopted children will go through a grieving process, but the intensity of the grief and when it is felt most, depend on the individual child and the age at which he was adopted. If children were adopted before the age of two, they will grieve for a fantasy mother. If they were adopted after the age of two, they might remember the separation or their immediate environment; in that case, children may not only feel sadness and anger, but they may also hope that the adoption is temporary and that the original bond will be re-established. Because intense sadness is mostly difficult and threatening to endure, many children may fall into a state of denial. They may stop asking questions about their adoption, but that certainly doesn't mean that they are not thinking about it.

Emotional development

At this age, children want to fit in with their peer group. Their social environment becomes more important to them. This means that they can experience their adoption as a burden. They look different, have different names and a different family composition compared to most of the children in their class. They don't look like their sister, their aunt or their father. Your child will probably try to hide his differences rather than emphasise them, so he may be less enthusiastic to talk about his adoption at home. Sometimes, it is helpful to children to share their adoptive status with their adoptive relatives or peers. An adoptive mother writes about the importance of this for her seven-year-old son:

> Richard (seven years) and Michael (nine years) travelled with us to China where we adopted our daughter, Yulin. When her nanny left, Yulin cried. Richard asked: 'Why is she doing that, Mum?' I said that she was sad because her nanny went away and Richard responded: 'So now she has been abandoned.' And then he said to his five-year-old brother: 'We were also abandoned, Michael.'

> After we arrived back home, Richard said to me: 'I am happy that Michael is my brother.' I said enquiringly: 'Yes?' Then Richard said: 'Yes, because Michael was also abandoned.' I said: 'You mean that you are happy that you and your brother have the same history, so that you can share your thoughts and feelings?' Richard said approvingly: 'Yes, I am!'

Children of this age are not only preoccupied with their social environment, but also with honesty and fairness. From the age of eight, many children will wonder how fair their adoption was, in comparison to orphaned children who were left behind. They may ask themselves whether they were placed with the "right" family, and fantasise about other adoptive parents. Many children also experience loyalty conflicts: they may feel that it isn't fair to their adoptive parents to talk about their birth parents, especially if they think this might upset you.

These are all reasons why your child might avoid talking about adoption at this age. Most probably, it is not because they are not interested, but it is because of their apprehension or uncertainty. Try to stay alert to this and keep the subject of adoption open for discussion; for example, you could praise your child's talents and mention that his birth parents probably gave him those talents. Try also to be particularly aware of your child on his official adoption day and on his birthday: you could ask him how he is feeling, what he is thinking, etc. If you know what is going on, you may anticipate his feelings and initiate a dialogue about his adoption.

Misinterpretations and fantasies

If I love my birth mother or think about her, then I love my adoptive parents less.

Children of this age often think that you cannot love two people at the same time, for example, girls often have only one best friend. Your child may experience a loyalty conflict: you adopted him and took care of him, you gave him lots of love and attention, and thanks to you he is doing well. He may feel ungrateful if he is curious or sad about his "other mother and father". Even if parents are very open about the adoption, children may have divided loyalties. It is important to recognise signals that may indicate an inner conflict.

You can help your child by explaining that love doesn't need to be exclusive, that each person is allowed to love more than one person at the same time. You could make this more meaningful by explaining that when you had your oldest child, you loved him, but that you loved his brother or sister just as much when he or she became part of the family. You could explain that some families have five children and that the mother and father love each and every one of them.

I have absolutely no problem with my adoption.
This can be a denial mechanism to block any feelings about the past. It makes sense that adopted children may want to deny any feeling of sadness; it can be very scary to feel intensely sad. Some adopted children find it difficult to get over this fear. If they allow themselves to feel the pain, they will have to face a very disturbing reality: parents never abandon their children, yet they were abandoned. As a young and innocent child, they were left alone in the world. Children who dare to face this will find it a painful experience, but only when they have been through this process can they begin to build their own identity.

It is important to recognise denial and fear but also to respect it. When your child is emotionally strong enough (some children take longer than others), he will most probably allow himself to feel sad. Always validate his sadness – in other words, give him a shoulder to cry on or just let him talk about his feelings while you listen.

If your child continues to deny his feelings of anger or sadness and you are anxious about his behaviour, you could ask for advice from an adoption counsellor. Your child may just be a straightforward, uncomplicated child who is not very preoccupied with his past. On the other hand, persistent denial may also mean that your child doesn't have enough basic trust to allow himself to feel the pain. Also, sometimes adopted children have such intense feelings about their past that they can only work through the pain of their relinquishment once they are emotionally mature. In such cases, the denial mechanism may be very functional.

My birth parents would understand me better than you do. They are probably much nicer.

Whether they are adopted or not, many children of this age have fantasies about other, more ideal parents. Many of them sometimes think that their parents are not the nicest people to live with. Their fantasies mostly vanish as they begin to learn that no one is perfect, including themselves and their parents. For adopted children, this is a completely different situation; the other parents they think of are their birth parents, who will not automatically disappear from their fantasies as they get older. On the contrary, because these parents live only in their imagination, the fantasy will persist and become more of a burden over the years. The only way adoptive parents can help is to accept that it is happening and to talk about these fantasies together with their child.

You can start doing this from the time your child is five or six, for example, on birthdays. You could bring the subject up on this day by saying: 'I can imagine that you think about your birth mother on your birthday. I also think about her quite a lot on this day.'

If your child wants to talk about it, you could also encourage him to draw a picture of his birth parents or to write them a letter. You can then keep them for him in a special box.

I have been lucky and don't deserve to be happy.

From about age seven or eight, adopted children are able to perceive conflicts relating to unfair situations in their native country and the world. As children progress through primary school, they think more about poverty – those who have and those who haven't – social justice – what's fair and what isn't – and oppression – who's strong and who's weak. Your child is now feeling part of the big world and he may find it difficult to accept that other children are not as lucky as he is. He may even believe that he doesn't deserve to be happy as well as lucky. This feeling of "survival guilt" may take on extreme forms. Some children stop eating, for example, or harm themselves; other children become depressed or aggressive.

You should prepare yourself for your child's political questions and growing social conscience. It may become very important to him to know that your interest in his native country did not stop when your wish for a child was fulfilled. Maybe he wants to start up a fund to send aid to his birth country. Try to help him with it. You could also start a project yourself by collecting gifts or clothes to send to his orphanage. Your child will get the feeling that you are involved with his birth country and that together you have made a small, personal contribution to a better world.

Frequently asked questions

From approximately 7 or 8 years old (maybe even younger):

- Why was I given up for adoption, given away?
- Didn't my mother love me?
- Wasn't I nice enough?
- Didn't she like me?
- What does she look like?
- Was my mother a nice mother?
- Is she my real mother (and you aren't)?
- Is my mother well? Is she still alive?
- Why didn't you give her any money?

Up to and including 12 years (or even older):

- Who was my father?
- Where is my father now? Is he still alive?
- Where is my mother now?
- How are my parents? What are they doing?
- What do they look like? Do they look like me?
- Do they think about me sometimes?

- Why couldn't they take care of me?
- Why couldn't my father stay with my mother?
- Do I have more family (brothers/sisters)?
- What do my brothers/sisters look like? Do they look like me?
- Why was I adopted and my brothers and sisters (or other children in the orphanage) were not? Have they been adopted now?
- Why are some people poor and other people rich?
- How much did you have to pay for me?
- Why didn't you give the money to my parents instead of taking me away?
- Why aren't you supporting them now?

Chapter 7 discusses in more detail the questions that adopted children ask, and how you might respond.

3

Telling your child the adoption story

The importance of being open

Adopted children will benefit from being raised in a family where adoption is discussed from a young age and in an open and understandable way. Keeping secrets about the past can damage their identity formation; it can also damage their trust in you.

If your child does not know the facts from an early age, she may, during primary school, make up wild fantasies about her birth parents or about the reasons why she was given up for adoption. She may also develop split feelings of loyalty between you and her birth parents. If adoptive parents don't, or very seldom, talk about the adoption, children might not know for sure whether they are allowed to ask or fantasise about their birth parents; they may think that it isn't fair to their adoptive parents. They may also start feeling scared that they may be abandoned or rejected again. During puberty, and later on in life, this insecurity can lead to an even greater confusion. By covering up the truth, you may be creating a vacuum where all the fantasies, thoughts and feelings collide together more and more furiously.

Holding back essential information creates "family secrets" that most probably will be unravelled some day, with all the unwelcome consequences. For instance, your young child may accidentally hear some of the facts from other people, and this could lead to inner withdrawal or to outwardly aggressive behaviour. If your child discovers the truth at an older age from documents, from someone else or (eventually) from you, she will have to rebuild her identity and her trust in you will inevitably be damaged.

If you want to build a strong bond with your child, you should be honest about her adoption history from the very moment she comes to live with you. This naturally doesn't mean that you tell a two-year-old the same story as you would tell a six- or eight-year-old. Toddlers have a very different reality to slightly older children or to children in primary school. They will therefore also have a different understanding of their adoption.

The importance of gathering information

Showing an interest in being open begins before and during the actual adoption. From the moment you receive the first details about your child, it is important that you collect as much information as possible about her medical and social history. Of course, there may be very little information available but try, in any case, to gather as much as you can.

- Before you travel to collect your child, make a list of questions you will want to ask the authorities, the staff in the institutions, the carers or the (foster) parents. What do you want to know about your child's birth, relinquishment, history, care, the environment, the family, etc?
- Remember that your child has the right to know as much as possible, so don't be put off by institutions that prefer not to share information with you. Don't be embarassed to offer a gift or money in order to visit the orphanage. Sometimes a doctor may be willing to provide information but was simply not asked to do so.

- Look around, photograph the environment, and try to speak to people who may know something about your child's past. Write down their names and addresses, and if they are related to your child, write down anything relating to their birth, their education, their health, their occupation, and so on (preferably with relevant dates).
- If your child was a foundling, try to track down any information that was circulated at the time your child was taken into care in an attempt to find the birth parents or other family members.
- When at home, you can continue searching for information through the internet or by contacting email groups of parents who have also adopted a child from the same region. You could possibly make contact with local authorities abroad and set up a donation project in order to stay in touch with the people in the birthplace of your child. It is precisely during these first years that information relating to your child and her birth family may be uncovered. These details will be very important to your child at a later stage.

What do I tell my child and at what age?

Many parents think that their toddlers and very young children will not be able to comprehend their adoption history, so parents put off the difficult moment of telling their child "the truth". However, parents often underestimate their child's level of understanding.

According to Bruner (quoted in Kohnstamm, 2002, pp. 106–107), you can, in principle, make everything understandable to a child if the information is adapted to their specific level of understanding. Bruner is also convinced that new vocabulary can lead to a new way of thinking. The more varied the language that is available to your child, the clearer her thoughts will be.

You can give your child a head start by talking freely about her adoption history from a very young age. In this way, your child will learn additional vocabulary and can learn about the relationship between the words and the reality. If she understands these relationships, then she can also have new thoughts about adoption. By doing this, your young child can register the truth and digest it before emotionally coming to terms with the adoption at a later stage. She will not suddenly have to be confronted with totally new information, because she already knows the facts, but from about age seven or eight, she will be able to focus on what she really feels. If there is openness and trust between you, she will not be troubled by questions like 'Is there any information that I am not aware of?', and 'Can I believe you?'

An additional reason to start talking to your child about her adoption at an early age is that it gives you the chance to practise telling a difficult story. Talking about it to a young child is easier because the facts have been simplified. You can slowly add a little more information without your child suddenly experiencing it as difficult or painful.

Another positive reason for starting this conversation at this stage is that it gives your child the signal that adoption is a valued subject and that she can talk about it whenever she wants to. The openness that you achieve by talking about the adoption at the beginning can be maintained and increased if you regularly talk about adoption to your child.

Babies and toddlers: 0–3-year-olds

You can tell a baby or toddler a very simple story about her adoption. Up to about the age of three, it is sufficient to make small references to the adoption or to the birth parents. You may look together at photos of the adoption journey and of the arrival. If a plane flies past, you could mention the journey. If you send photos to the orphanage or foster parents, you could actively involve your child by letting her add some stickers or drawings or by helping you decide which pictures you should send. You can also regularly tell her how happy you were when she came to live with you.

It is enough to tell a child of about three years old that she was in another "nice woman's tummy". Toddlers (and slightly older children) can find it scary if they hear that they were in a strange woman's tummy. If you add that it was a "nice" woman, your child might feel more comforted. According to Holly van Gulden and Lisa Bartels-Rabb (2001, p. 190), parents should ensure that, when speaking about the birth parents, they always include feelings in the dialogue. This will give the birth parents a more human dimension.

Up to the age of four or five, the fact that your child is an adopted child is not really interesting to her. During this first stage, the important thing is to tell her she was included in the family through adoption (and that other children are included in a family through birth). In other words, an adopted toddler should first learn that only the way in which she became part of a family is different and that, in all other aspects, she is the same as other children in other families. You could tell a toddler that she was adopted from a far-away country and that she was brought home on a plane, or that you both (if there's two of you) wanted a child very much and were very happy when she became part of the family.

Some psychologists recommend that parents should only start talking about adoption to children from about the age of five. According to them, children younger than this cannot understand precisely what adoption is. They can then regard their adoptive status as something that makes them different to others, with the consequence that adopted children can develop a negative self-image. According to Lois Ruskai Melina, this risk is not as great if parents talk about adoption 'as something included in the family' (2001, Chapter 2). The question of what adoption actually means does not need to be discussed before the age of five.

It is important from the beginning to think carefully about the language you will use when talking about adoption. How you refer to your child's birth parents is particularly important. A toddler might find it very confusing if you speak about the mother whose tummy they were in. For very young children, the terms "mother"/"mum" or "father"/"dad" refer only to the two adults who care for them on a daily basis. They are not yet able to understand which principle allows them to call two different women "mother" or "mum". It is better to indicate a clear distinction, for example, to talk about your "birth mother/father", or "Colombian mother/father", "Chinese mother/father". Although you still use the words father or mother, there is a difference, and this enables your child to distinguish between them. Some parents prefer to talk about the woman who gave birth to their child, but many adopters feel that this is too distant. You could also choose to call the birth mother the "nice woman who gave birth to you". If you know the names of the birth parents, you can refer to them by name – doing so will make them seem more real. The more human you can make your child's birth parents seem, the safer your child will feel to have two sets of parents.

If you do not know their names, you could ask your child if she wants to choose a name for her birth parents. An adoptive mother told me how she and her sons thought of a name:

> Tonight, while sitting at the dinner table, Richard (five) and Michael (seven) started talking about the woman in Haïti who gave birth to them. Because I am never sure what I should call their birth mother, I thought, I am going to ask the boys. So, I asked: 'What would you like to call this woman?' I gave them a few examples, like tummy mother, birth mother. Then Michael said: 'I know! Princess Marguerita!' Both boys started laughing. We laughed together for a little longer but finally decided what it should be. The boys chose "Haïti mother".

You may want to be even more open during the later toddler phase. Although your child probably still won't understand much about what you are telling her, openness shouldn't be a problem. Keep it simple, tell the truth only to a certain extent; talk about it the way it is, and then at a later stage, add further details. According to

Melina, you could, for example, say this:

> Mummy and Daddy wanted a baby very much but we couldn't make one ourselves. You were made by another man and woman and you grew inside the other woman and were born to her just like other children are. Those people are called your birth mother and birth father.
>
> But your birth mother and birth father couldn't take care of a baby, so after you were born, you came to live with us. I am sure they were sad that they were separated from you and you were probably sad too, although you don't remember that. I was also sad that you weren't born to me, but now we're happy that we're a family.
> (2001, p. 29)

Melina writes that parents establish an important base by telling the above story, which every parent can adapt or embellish. At a later stage, parents can add more detailed information:

- You have identified your motives for adopting. It is important that your child realises that you had needs too that were met by the adoption; it wasn't done as a charitable act.
- You have acknowledged the important role both birth parents had in the creation of your child and have presented them in a realistic but empathetic way.
- By saying the birth parents couldn't take care of a baby, you have suggested why they decided to place their child for adoption; this places responsibility for the decision on them, and not on the child. There wasn't anything about the child that made her more difficult to care for than other babies. This will be more important later on when your child will realise that most children are not placed for adoption, and will wonder whether the adoption took place because there was something wrong with her.
- You have told your child that she was conceived, grew inside her

birth mother, and was born, just like all children. This will also be more important later on when she comes to understand reproduction.
- You have acknowledged that there are feelings associated with adoption and that some of them are good feelings and some of them are sad or angry feelings.'
(2001, pp. 29–30)

Your child may feel that she should be grateful to you for adopting her. If you did not adopt due to infertility, or if you already had one or more birth children, you could say:

> *We wanted another child in the family.*

or

> *We specifically wanted to adopt a child and not have another child born to us.*

Later, you could add:

> *It didn't make any difference to us whether a child grew in my tummy or not. You were already there and you needed a new mum and dad; we wanted to care for you rather than for another child of our own.*

> *If I'd had my own child, then I wouldn't have had you!*

Young children: 3–7-year-olds

Young children can absorb more information although, until the age of six or seven, they have only a basic understanding of adoption. Most young children will not have negative feelings about their adoption before this age. They don't yet understand that almost all children live with their birth parents, and even if they do, they are probably not preoccupied with it. Young children live in the present and they accept what they experience; they can't imagine that it could be any different.

The first questions about the birth mother and how your child grew in her tummy will probably be asked around age four or five. You might feel surprised because a question like 'Why did my birth mother give me up for adoption?' sounds so profound that it seems like your child wants to hear the whole story. However, this is not the case – at this stage, she is asking for only a very small piece of the puzzle. The following answers will mostly suffice for this age group:

> *She couldn't look after you when you were born.*

> *She didn't have enough money.*

> *Your mother was still very young.*

Or (applicable to China):

> *She was only allowed to have one or two children, but sometimes parents have more children than allowed.*

If you don't know the answer, you could say:

> *We don't know, but I am sure that your birth mother gave you up for adoption because she had no other choice.*

You can tell your child that you can search for answers together when she is older.

Children of this age can't identify with adult motives – the child sees everything from an egocentric perspective. To avoid confusion, talk about the reasons for her adoption in a very simple manner and tell your child regularly that she wasn't adopted because she was naughty or unwanted.

Parents who have adopted a disabled child must be particularly aware of children's beliefs that they were rejected because they were "not perfect" or because they were "not healthy". Some children might think that they were "saved" by their adoptive parents because they had a life-threatening disease and that they should always "be thankful". It is vital to explain to your child that her birth parents did not give her up for adoption because they didn't love her, but because they were not ready or capable of caring for a child with a disability. You can also explain to your child that her birth parents probably didn't have the money to pay for an operation or for treatment, or that these operations could not be performed in their native country, and that treatment was not available. In this way, you are not judging her birth parents. Your child should know that she was not only wanted by you but that, despite everything, she was also treasured by her birth parents. By explaining the possible reasons for the adoption, you can also reassure your child that in no way should she feel responsible for it.

Children in primary school: 7–12-year-olds

Children in primary school can comprehend more complex reasons to explain why they were given up for adoption. They are capable of understanding that their birth father and mother had "financial difficulties" or "a bad marriage", that their mother was "too young to raise a child", that their parents "were not married when they were born" or that they are "not alive".

However, it is still difficult for children at this level to really grasp the whole story. Your child may have been the third or fourth child in her family and the only one who was adopted, or the birth of your child might have brought shame to the birth family. If your child finds a story hard to understand, she may ask to hear it time and time again. It is hard to grasp reasons for adoption like 'the country's culture forcing a birth mother to do so', or 'birth parents only being able to care for three children and not for four'. As a result, your child may imagine that you don't dare to tell her the truth or that there was something really wrong with her when she was a baby.

It is important that you emphasise every time that there was nothing wrong with her and that it was not her fault that she was placed for adoption. Take note of your child's behaviour – if she doesn't want to see her baby photos, it may be because she feels that she looked very strange when she was born.

Be aware that, at this age, your child may be sad when you talk to her about adoption or the reasons for being given up for adoption. The best thing you can do is to accept her sadness – she is probably too young to understand the personal, political or cultural situation. Validate her feelings by neutrally stating: 'You possibly don't want to see the photos because you think that you looked strange as a baby.'

Even if you are not sure about the reasons for her sad or distant behavior, a statement like this can lead somewhere. Your child will probably confirm or deny your assumptions and in this way you may be able to start a conversation about the subject. It is helpful to make a statement rather than question your child. If you ask a question, your child will probably give no answer or an unclear one (see Chapter 5).

Tell your child if she is misinterpreting the situation and try to explain it to her. Let her see for herself by showing her photos, medical or social reports.

Try to translate complicated information into scenarios your child can relate to. For example, you could give her one or two dolls that she must care for day and night. She will realise herself how difficult that is and how much time and dedication it requires to look after a child. Or you might say: 'Imagine that no one will talk to you...how would you feel?' This may be comparable to the situation of a birth mother who will be rejected by her family if she doesn't have her child adopted. In Chapter 4, I give more examples to help you translate complicated and painful information. Always emphasise that the birth parents were responsible for the situation and not your child.

It is important that you pay attention to the consistency of all versions of the adoption story that you tell your child from a young age. The story must be told in such a way that more and more details can be added, depending on the developmental stage of your child. You should not say things that you will have to change at a later stage. You could write down a step-by-step story that matches the facts and keeps pace with the emotional and intellectual development of your child (see Chapter 2).

The true story

Adopted children are always curious about their past. If your child is very young, this curiosity will be only mild, but most children realise, at some point, that the information about their past is very important to them. Ensure that your child eventually has access to as much of the information as you have. Generally, it is best to tell your adopted child everything about her past before she reaches puberty (approximately 11 or 12 years). There are various reasons for this.

- Children listen less to their parents during puberty. Your child may more quickly distance herself from you as a "giver of bad news"; there is even a chance that at this age she might not believe the information you are giving her.
- Puberty is a stage when a person's identity is well formed. It is much better for her to have heard the whole truth at a younger age, so that she does not have to redefine her identity over and over again.
- If you have not told her the whole story by the age of 12, then you will be faced with a dilemma, for when *are* you going to tell her? You may delay telling her the truth for years because she is busy with so many other things or because it's hard to "get through to her". These may seem like good reasons but Vera Fahlberg, a widely

respected US adoption professional, warns against the pitfalls: according to her it is a difficult task in itself for adopted children 'to move out of the house because many adopted individuals have a resurgence of feelings of abandonment as they approach moving away from home and family. It is important that the information about their origins...not be associated with the experience of parent separation and loss (even though this time the separation is developmentally appropriate)' (Fahlberg, quoted in Keefer and Schooler, 2000, p. 110).

- To tell your child the "real story" just as she is going to live independently is not the best time to do so: she needs the support of the family while working through painful information.
- Telling the facts at an early age is also important for building a basis of trust between you and your child. By hearing the whole truth (in phases and depending on age), your child will learn that she can always trust you. This bond of trust may also affect her self-confidence. She is hearing painful facts (perhaps with the help of an adoption specialist) and at the same time, you are demonstrating to her that you love her unconditionally and that she can count on your support.

If you are unsure as to what you should say, or if you have doubts because the information is too painful, you should contact an adoption therapist. It is not an absolute rule that parents have to communicate everything to their child before the age of 12. But in most cases, it is better for both parties if the truth has been told before the onset of puberty.

General advice

- Do not wait until your child starts asking questions about her adoption. Most children will not initiate discussion themselves, and your child could know almost nothing by the time she is six or seven years old. She may then hear something from other people. Children before the age of six or seven "register" the story of their adoption; they will probably have very few or no negative feelings about it if you are positive. It is a good time to tell the basic facts.

- Be careful about saying that the birth mother could not take care of a child properly. If children search for their birth parents, they may find that the parents together, or each with a different partner now, *have* other children whom they have taken good care of. Always add that it was *because of the situation at that time* that your child was given up for adoption.

- If the birth mother was too young to take care of her child, try to explain to your child that people's bodies are able to give birth to a child long before they are properly able to look after a child. Tell her that her birth mother was *at that time not ready to be a mother to any baby* – perhaps she was even still at school. You could also explain that you need a certain amount of maturity and experience to be a mother, and that you need to lead a stable life.

- Ask your child what she thinks it takes to be a good father or mother. Many children will say: 'You have to love your child and you need money.' You could than ask if she thinks that money and love is all you need. You could make a list together of other things that are important to raise a child properly, for instance: 'You also need a lot of patience'; 'You have to teach a child what is right and wrong'; 'Parents must help their children make good choices'; 'Parents teach their children to be caring and loving so that later on in life they can care for themselves and love someone else.' Whatever else you both think of, it is also important to explain that some people aged 19 can take care of a child and other people, at the age of 30, are still unable to be good parents.

- Try to distinguish between the birth parents' behaviour and their value as people. Your child will most probably feel a strong bond with her birth parents. If she has the feeling that they are bad people, she might conclude that she is also a bad person (see Chapter 1, *I can't handle that my child was abandoned/mistreated*).

- Avoid saying that the birth mother loved your child so much that she gave her up for adoption. Your child could make the logical connection that you might also give her up because you also love her very much. It is better to say that the birth mother probably loved your child very much but, at that time in her life, she couldn't take care of a child. She wanted the best, and that is why she gave her up for adoption. Reassure her that she will never be given up for adoption again.

- If you tell your child that her birth parents probably think about her often, it is important to bear in mind that the actual situation might be quite different. They may not think about her at all. Some birth parents deliberately cut off from their child. This can be for cultural or social reasons, or because the birth parents are in denial or are addicted to drugs or to alcohol. You could say: 'I can't imagine that your birth parents don't think of you.' In this way you avoid the possibility of disappointment for your child later on in life.

- Young children can only concentrate for very short periods. It may be difficult to assess whether you have told a piece of their story at the right moment. Maybe you were telling your child something important about her adoption and she just jumped off your lap to go and play. If your child does not ask questions and immediately starts doing something else, if doesn't necessarily mean that she has no interest in what you have said – your child might have been busy doing something or perhaps you interrupted her while she was playing. She may need time to digest the information and she might come back to you a few days later to talk about something you told her. If she doesn't, it may mean that she isn't interested for the time being in what you have said, but it may also mean that the message has had a deep impact and she needs to deny the truth to herself.

- Try not to force the subject of adoption, but at the same time, ensure that you pay an appropriate amount of attention to your child's history, preferably during natural, calm in-between moments, such as while you are washing the dishes or on special days that are linked to the adoption (see also Chapter 6).

- Don't be surprised if your child is confused about her adoption even though you have explained it very carefully. An adoptive father wrote to me:

> We had explained to our son very often what adoption meant. However, when we were moving to another house, he suddenly asked us whether he was now also going to get a new dad and mum.

- A trip to their country of origin before the onset of puberty can be quite a "freeing" experience for your child. It is, however, important to find out whether your child really wants to go, and that she is not just trying to please you.
Children who travel to their native country at a young age learn about it in an unforced way. They are able to discover how far they feel at home in each of their two countries. They may also be able to visit the orphanage where they stayed, their foster parents, or even their birth family.

- From about age 9–12, children usually become increasingly interested in their birth parents. Unfortunately, it often isn't possible to get to know them, and if your child was adopted from abroad, you may not even know their names. If the circumstances surrounding the birth and adoption are such that you can reveal their identities in a responsible manner, you could consider whether you should do so before you take your child back to her native country.

- Children who are adopted after the age of two (and sometimes even before this age) often have memories of their stay in the native country. However painful some of them may be, children carry these memories with them either consciously or unconsciously. If your child is able to share them with you, she may be able to put her memories into perspective.

- It is possible that your child will use direct, hurtful words when describing bad memories or strong feelings. Try not to correct her language – children are able to let you know how they are feeling by the language they use. If you try to re-phrase it more positively or less directly, your child might think that she is not being taken seriously or that you are denying her feelings.

- If your child says that she hates her birth parents, it is important that you actively accept these feelings. You may be inclined to dismiss her negative views and to re-frame them in a more positive way, but it is better to not do this. Name her negative feelings and validate them, but don't say that you share them. Tomorrow she might tell you that she actually does love her birth father and mother. These fluctuations from one extreme to another are quite normal. By giving words to her different feelings, she is able to work through her emotions. If you express negative feelings towards her birth parents, she could begin to have negative feelings about you.

- Try not to judge the information about your child's past. It is up to your child to judge this information for herself.
- You may want to discuss important points with your partner or another trustworthy person before you talk to your child. You could also record what you want to say and listen to how it sounds. If you practise, you might find it easier to choose the right words.
- If your child is going through a stressful time (getting a new brother/sister, moving to a new house, attending a new school, dealing with an operation, a long-term illness, the death of a loved one or a divorce), try not to confront her with new information related to the adoption. She probably needs all her energy to get through the current situation. It can, however, be good to go over adoption information that she already knows. During a stressful period, your child may think more about her birth parents or experience a stronger fear of abandonment.
- Try to be more alert on special or celebratory days, especially if these days are related to the adoption, for example, the day that she joined your family, your child's birthday (this day can be a painful reminder of the day she was born), Father's Day or Mother's Day. On these occasions, you might be able to find out how she feels about the adoption and about her birth parents and what she remembers about the time she spent in her native country. Your child will probably respond emotionally and with sadness, but if you offer her the opportunity to express her feelings, she may then be able to feel happy a few hours later.

In general, it is the adoptive parents themselves who can best guide their child through their past. Try to create a safe environment, so that your child will feel safe enough to start a dialogue about painful subjects (see Chapter 5).

If you are apprehensive about your child's emotions or your own ability to deal with her pain, you could ask for advice from a specialist. Often parents have a reliable intuition about whether a child needs additional help or not. If your child has a traumatic past, you should ask a specialist for advice, even if your child does not seem to remember anything.

Approaching teachers at school

School is an important environment for your adopted child, as it is for any child.

- When your child first goes to school, you could make a little book about her adoption, using simple sentences and a few photos to tell the story of where your child comes from and when and why she was adopted. Your child may want to pass the book around for everyone to see. In this way, the other children can get a first impression of what it means to be adopted.
- As your child gets older, you may want to make another book together, which includes more information about the adoption. Your child may want to tell her story on her adoption day or on another suitable occasion.
- Don't expect teachers to know a lot about adoption. You can help them by giving them books and brochures to read, although they may never have the time to read them. BAAF also has a guide for young children about adoption – this could be helpful for other children at school to learn about adoption (Shah, 2003). It may be more effective to provide the teacher(s) with short, specific information about your child's recent adoption-related development: write down, for example, what your child understands about her past, the adoption vocabulary you use together, to what extent your child is preoccupied with information about her adoption and how this affects her. Explain to the teacher the confusion your child may experience as a result of comments made by children and teachers at school. Point out, if necessary, any specific behaviour of your child that is related to the grieving process at the moment. This can be written down on several handouts and, if necessary, added to during the school year. One advantage of producing handouts is that all your child's teachers can have the same information directly from you.

- If it is difficult for a teacher to communicate with your child, consider giving concrete examples of what works well at home, such as paying close attention, making a lot of eye contact, and praising even small achievements. Write down, if you think it necessary, what doesn't work with your child, again with concrete examples which illustrate your points.
- Instead of providing handouts, you could use a "to-and-from" notebook. The teacher can respond to your observations with his or her own, and all the information can be kept together. You could then pass on this notebook to a new teacher at the beginning of the next school year. When going from one school year to the next, you could fill in what happened that was relevant during the holidays.
- Teachers may have a great impact on your child's development. Children who are grieving (see Chapters 8 and 9) or who have insufficient basic trust will do better if they feel safe with their teacher and if they get the chance to share their feelings and thoughts with him or her.
- Ask the teacher not to share information about the adoptive status of your child with the class unless you know that they are planning to do so. Arrange with him or her to talk it over with you and your child beforehand. If your child is going through a difficult stage, it would be better not to disclose certain things in class. Perhaps you could be present whenever this topic is discussed so that you are able to answer questions and support your child.
- Your child will naturally participate in lessons about other countries and this might spontaneously lead to a discussion about adoption. This need not be a problem, and anyway it is difficult to avoid. Ask the teacher to let you know, so that you can be aware if your child is excited, quiet, angry or sad when she comes home.
- Your child is, of course, a "normal child": she is made like all other children. However, her background is far from what others are used to. Although teachers (and possibly other parents or classmates) may suggest that 'these days so many children have unusual family situations', the situation of your child does not compare at all to those of divorced or single parents. Assure the teacher that you think it is great if everything is going well, but that in terms of your

child's behaviour and achievements, she cannot always be treated like every other child – at times, she will be preoccupied with her background.

- If your child does not yet have basic trust, tell the teacher that your child will benefit most from a positive environment. According to Gray (2002), it is important that teachers are encouraged to make seven positive remarks for one negative remark. The ratio negative: positive should be ideally 1:7.

- Ask the teacher to inform you about any planned projects that are related to family structures. The teacher might, for instance, ask the children to bring in baby photos of themselves. If your child has no baby photos, tell the teacher, and also explain if your child doesn't know anything about herself as a baby or toddler. Maybe other good alternative assignments could be suggested for the whole class. Children could bring their favorite toddler photo to school and then say something about it to the class.

- If children are going to make a family tree at school, this is probably not a problem until children are aged six or seven. The purpose of making a family tree at this age is mostly to make children aware of the bond with their parents. Unless your child has other ideas, birth parents can be left out. Perhaps she would like to put the date when you became her parents next to your names.

- If a family tree has to be produced towards the end of primary school, think of a way to include the genetic bond with the birth parents and share your ideas with the teacher. It is important that both the birth parents and the adoptive parents are represented, as well as any birth brothers and sisters. Van Gulden and Bartels-Rabb visualise the family tree of an adopted child as different houses and not as a tree (2001, p. 244). The nice thing about using different houses is that this can show children that parents were once children themselves and were part of a family, and that when they got married and had their own children, they moved to another house.

The importance of privacy

Almost all adoptive parents agree that the details included in background reports about their child are their child's personal information. However, there are still differences of opinion about how much of this information should be accessible to family and friends. Femmie Juffer says in this regard:

> Some adoptive parents feel there should be no secrets about their child's background. They talk about the details to family and friends. They intend to pass the facts on to their child in the same way later on. Other parents feel that the background report contains much personal information that belongs to their child. They feel that it is private and that the child should be the first one to hear it. When the child is old enough and knows her own story, people can ask her about it. She can then decide whether she wants to answer the questions or not.
>
> We don't know which approach is better or more responsible in terms of the well-being of the child. It seems, however, important that parents are aware of this choice and that they make a well-considered decision. No matter which alternative they choose, they should respect the adoption information about their child as personal information.
> (1999, p. 108)

Depending on the choice you make, consider the following points:

- If you don't want to share painful information with family or good friends, then you could explain to them that if the information was about yourself, you would share it with them willingly, but that since you have learnt about adoption, you realise that you don't have the right to share this information because it belongs to your child. She will have to decide in her own time how much she wants to share.

- If you do share painful background information about your child with teachers or close family before sharing it with your child, the chances are that she might hear it first from others. Make sure that they will not pass on this information to anyone else, not to other children, friends or colleagues. You should say clearly what adoption information they are allowed to share with others because this information is available to the whole family.
- If the school holds confidential information about your child, ask them to return it to you at the end of each school year. Explain that you will personally provide the new teacher with up-to-date information relating to the background of your child.
- Be careful not to give older brothers or sisters information that your child doesn't yet know. You can't expect children to keep secrets.
- If you decide not to share any or very little information with others, be careful not to become obsessive about it. There are many aspects of adoption information that you can share with loved ones while your child is present. You can, for example, talk generally about the birth country and the social context in which children are being given up for adoption. Always try to talk about it positively and involve your child in the conversation. She should learn that it isn't threatening to talk about adoption and that it can even be pleasant and interesting. But only share information with friends and family that your child already knows, and always answer questions without giving away something that your child doesn't yet know.

Conclusion

In this chapter, I have discussed how you can fill in the gaps about your child's adoption story at different stages. The next chapter discusses how to talk about very painful information with your child.

Although being open is important, you should also realise that openness is not a "formula" for taking away your child's adoption-related pain. Even if you have been totally open about the adoption and have carefully explained to your child why she was given up for adoption, she will, from her seventh or eighth year, feel periodically angry and sad about the fact that she was relinquished at a young age.

By creating an open atmosphere, where adoption conversations can take place, your child can learn that she doesn't need to be afraid or ashamed of her feelings. In Chapter 5, I discuss communication techniques to help your child to be less afraid to talk about her feelings.

4

Sharing difficult information with your child

Once again: the importance of being open

Sometimes it is very difficult to explain to adopted children what it means to be adopted. It is even more difficult to have to confront your child with painful reasons as to why they were given up for adoption. You probably want to wait a little longer before sharing such distressing information with your child. If your child was traumatised while living in his birth country, you might be inclined to shield him from frightening memories for several years. In both cases, you probably want to spare your child confusion and intense sadness for as long as possible.

However, it is very important that you are open about painful information from the beginning, while being aware of the emotional development of your child as well as his level of understanding. It might sound contradictory, but children are often relieved when they learn the whole truth, especially if it includes disturbing circumstances. They may have vague memories or feelings connected to the period when they lived in their birth country, which have possibly been in their minds (consciously or unconsciously) for months or years. Once these children hear what actually happened, they often understand their feelings better; they may then eventually realise why they have been feeling fearful or insecure for years.

As well as being open about the painful reasons for adoption, it is important to search for as much information as possible about your child, preferably during the adoption process, especially for a child who has had traumatic experiences. If you are able to, also try to discover something positive in your child's history, as this can have great significance when he gets older.

This chapter explains how to handle painful information in a supportive way. I have based this mainly on the work of Keefer and Schooler (2000, Chapter 8).

Being abandoned

Thousands of intercounty adopted children are foundlings and in most cases there is not much more information available about their origins, apart from the date on which the child was found. The birth parents are unknown and there is usually no possibility of obtaining more information about the period before the child was abandoned. Only very seldom do parents leave a note with their child giving the exact date of birth or the reason why the child was abandoned.

Even if parents of foundlings can't tell their children anything about their birth parents or their history, it is still important that these children hear the facts about their adoption from a young age, and that you provide as much information as possible. Important points that you could say to your child are:

- It wasn't your fault that you had to leave your birth mother (father).
- You were most likely warmly dressed and left in a place where nice people would find you.
- Your mother could not take care of a baby at that stage of her life.
- I can understand if you sometimes feel angry or sad because you

don't know anything about your birth parents.
- I can tell you something about your birth country and why parents sometimes think that adoption is best for their child, even when in their hearts they don't want to give their child up.

You can give your child some concrete information, depending on their age and phase of development.

3–5-year-olds

> *Your birth mother could not take care of you. She wanted you to be safe. So she probably dressed you warmly and chose a place where lots of people passed by. She knew if she left you there, someone would find you quickly and take you to a place where you would be well looked after and where you might get a new mum and dad.*

5–8-year-olds

> *We find it very sad that we know nothing about your birth parents. Maybe you also feel sad or angry that you don't know anything about them. You must understand that it isn't your fault that you had to leave your birth mother.*

If your child comes from China, you could say:

> *Your birth parents couldn't keep you because they were only allowed to have one or two children.*

Depending on your child's level of understanding and interests, you could add:

> *Sometimes Chinese people have more children, and if they keep them all, they are punished (fined) because their government has to make sure that not too many children are born, otherwise there won't be enough food for all the people in China.*

Other reasons why people abandon their children could depend on the political or social situation of their birth country. You may only be able to speculate about this, but there are probably specific reasons why children are being abandoned in your child's country of origin:

> *Your parents very likely couldn't look after you because they didn't have enough money.*

> *Your mother may have been very young when you were born. Maybe that's why she couldn't look after you. She was still a child herself and perhaps she had no one to help her. She couldn't cope with the responsibility of raising her child properly.*

> *Your mother may have been single. In some countries it is very difficult to bring up a child on your own. Single mums often can't find work and then they can't feed their children.*

8–10-year-olds

At this age, you could talk about the social, cultural and/or economic aspects of your child's birth country and make it clear why his birth parents had to abandon him. The conversation could begin as it did when he was younger:

> *Sometimes I think about your birth parents. I find it sad that we know nothing about them. Maybe you also feel angry or sad sometimes because you'd like to know more about them.*

You could build on this by saying:

> *I could tell you something about your birth country, and why it is that in your native country fathers and mothers sometimes have to abandon their child, even though in*

their hearts they don't want to.

You could consider visiting your child's birth country at this stage. The connection with their birth country is often the only connection foundlings have with their roots. The advantage of visiting the native country at a young age may be that your child can get to know and experience his country in an easiser way than he would when he is older. It may also help him to replace his fantasies with the reality. Be aware that this trip might also cause your child some confusion and adoption-related grief, but you should accept that he will have to deal with this at some point in his young life, and that it is probably better for him to do so now than during puberty.

However, before making arrangements, it is important to find out whether your child really wants to visit his birth country, or whether he is only trying to please you. Adopted children often first start to grieve when they are in primary school (see Chapters 8 and 9) but your child might want to keep his adoption at the back of his mind for a while longer.

If your child is interested in his birth country, consider whether he can also learn to speak the language. Of course, this will depend on the language and on his ability to learn.

10–12-year-olds

Keep talking about the birth country so that your child can identify with his cultural and ethnic background. Confirm your child's feelings about his adoption periodically, and try to have conversations about it.

Also try to ensure that your child gets enough opportunities to be in contact with other adopted children, preferably from the same country, so that they can exchange experiences and talk about their feelings. If you have not yet visited his birth country, try to do so now.

Neglect/prostitution as a result of an addiction

Some children are relinquished for adoption because the birth mother or father was addicted to drugs or alcohol, which meant that the parents neglected their child, and maybe also became involved in prostitution or drug dealing. Sometimes such children may have been left to their fate; they may have been wandering the streets for months or years. Often they are taken away from their parents by the local police or child protection authorities. It is important to realise that children who are older when they are placed with new families will have memories of this time, even if they are not able to describe them in words. It is very important for them to be able to express themselves over time; your child may be able to share his memories, for example, by making drawings, through play or by talking about it. Even if your child has no memories of this period because he was too young, it is important to start talking about the past from about age six or seven; children often have fantasies or vague feelings about this period.

Neglected children have often been exposed for long periods to a fearful, uncertain situation because their unpredictable parents were never there when they needed them. Points that you can say and discuss are:

- It is not because of you that your birth mother (father) was addicted.
- You mustn't think that your birth mother (father) neglected you because she did not love you. It was because she was an addict and couldn't think clearly.
- Your birth mother (father) couldn't control her own life in order to give you a loving, safe home. Children should always grow up in a safe place.
- We will never leave you and we are always here for you if you need us.

Concrete information to tell your child could include the following:

3–5-year-olds

Your birth mother (or father) could not look after you properly. She was sick and had to sleep a lot. Mothers and fathers must take very good care of their small children. They must feed them and make sure they are always safe and never left alone. Your birth mother was not ready to be a mother when you were born. She had no husband or grandparents to help her. Other people found a safe home for you, with another mum and dad who could look after you every day, and that is why you are with us now.

From age four or five, you can begin with a simple explanation of addiction.

Your birth mother (or father) took a bad medicine. Not the kind of medicine you get from the doctor. She bought it from someone on the street. She thought she would feel happier if she took the medicine, but she only felt better for a short time. After a while she got sick and then she couldn't look after you very well.

5–8-year-olds

At age five and six you could explain the following:

A long time before you were born, your birth mother (or father) didn't feel good so she bought drugs/alcohol to make her feel better. At first she felt better so she thought the drugs were good for her. But they were not good for her because she couldn't think clearly and so she couldn't take care of you properly. In the end, you were safer with other people.

When your child is about seven years old, you could give an even more detailed description of addiction.

Drugs are very addictive, and this means that once you start taking them, you must use them every day, otherwise you feel sick or unhappy. In the beginning, your birth mother (or father) did feel better by taking drugs/alcohol, and then she started needing more and more. Nobody told her that, after a while, drugs just make you feel worse and more sick. Very quickly after she started taking the drugs, she had to buy more and more, but they were so expensive that she sometimes didn't have enough money left to buy food. You got less and less to eat and you didn't have warm clothes or a clean bed. The drugs made your birth mother sleep during the day, so she couldn't look after you any more. She wanted to, but she couldn't because she couldn't live without drugs/alcohol. She didn't realise that she had become addicted. You needed a mum and dad to take good care of you. That's why you are with us now forever.

8–12-year-olds

Some children at about age ten or 11 are ready to hear more detailed information. Try to find out if your child has questions that he doesn't dare to ask. What does he remember about his early life? What fantasies does he have? How does he feel about it?

Your birth mother (or father) was addicted to drugs/alcohol because she listened to the wrong people; because of this she started doing the wrong things and made the wrong decisions. Maybe you still remember a little about that time; I can imagine that you must have felt very sad or scared. If you would like to talk about it some time, or if you want to know more about it, you can always come to us. It's OK to ask peculiar questions or to share strange memories or feelings.

If the addicted birth mother earned her money through prostitution, you could talk to your child about it from about the age of nine or ten.

> *Your birth mother was addicted to drugs so she couldn't find work. Probably nobody wanted to give her a job, because she couldn't get to work on time or she didn't go to work because the drugs made her sick. She probably couldn't work very well and lost jobs. But she still needed drugs, so she had to find another way to earn money. She became a prostitute. Prostitutes sell their bodies to men they don't know. These men go to bed with them for money and then leave. (That is how your mother got pregnant with you.) Your mother wanted to look after you forever, but she couldn't because she had to have more money for drugs. So she went back to the streets to look for men who wanted to have sex with her for money. At these times, she left you all alone and that was bad for you. The neighbours called the police. They wanted you to be safe always.*

Depression/mental illness

Children who were given up for adoption because their birth parents were chronically depressed often have memories of the time when they lived with their birth father and/or mother. Perhaps the mother was always there, but she only sat and stared out of the window with a blank look on her face or she just stayed in bed so that the home was totally disorganised. There may have been days when the father or mother had radical mood swings and your child never knew if he had done something right or something wrong. One day he might have been locked in his room for a minor misdemeanour, whereas the next day he was allowed to behave as he liked.

Even though these children have lived in chaotic, unpredictable and sometimes even fearful circumstances, they may still love their birth parents very much. They may ask their adoptive parents over and over again why they couldn't have stayed with their own father and mother. Points to pay attention to and discuss are the following.

- Your birth mother/father could not think clearly or make good decisions. But that doesn't mean that they don't love you. They tried to look after you, but they couldn't.
- In the end, it was important for you to have a family where you would be safe and well cared for, where you could go to school and play with friends.
- Your birth mother/father didn't get sick because you were born. She was already sick long before you were born.
- I can imagine that you must be concerned about your birth mother/father. If you have questions about them, I will always answer them if I can.

Some concrete information you can give to your child is detailed below.

3–5-year-olds

Your birth mother (father) was sick when she gave you up for adoption. She needed other people to care for her. Sometimes she had good days and felt happy; but she also had bad days and then she felt very unhappy and couldn't take care of you. You needed parents who could take care of you every day so that nothing would happen to you. Your mother probably really wanted to look after you, but she couldn't. And that is why you are with us.

5–8-year-olds

At age five or six, you can repeat the story above (three–five years). From age seven or eight, you could go into more detail about the reasons for being adopted:

Your birth mother (or father) couldn't look after herself properly and therefore she couldn't look after you either. She wasn't well enough to do what other people can do. If you couldn't do your homework because you didn't understand it, you would probably ask us, your brother or your teacher for help. When your birth mother (or father) had problems, she got frightened and didn't know what to do. She probably asked nobody for help. If you don't do anything to solve your problems, then the problems get bigger. Think of what would happen if you never asked anyone to help you: if you didn't do your homework, you might not move up to the next grade. Your birth mother (father) often didn't understand how things happen and how to solve problems. Your birth mother couldn't think clearly because she was mentally ill. Her mind was ill, not her body. There are medicines to help people who are mentally ill; but your mother didn't get well enough to keep you safe. That is why you are with us now.

8–12-year-olds

Your birth mother (or father) was mentally ill; she suffered from depression for a long time (or she had another illness, for example, schizophrenia). She was ill long before you were born. Everyone gets sick sometimes, but most of us get a headache, a toothache or influenza. But your birth mother/father got ill in her mind so that she couldn't think clearly any longer. Because of her illness, she couldn't work and she couldn't take care of her children properly. She also had to go to the hospital quite often for her medicines so that she could start feeling better and happier again. Maybe sometimes you are worried about your birth mother/father. If you have questions about them, I will always answer them if I can.

Abuse

Sometimes children have lived in an orphanage where they have been treated unkindly; sometimes children have been abused by their birth parents or staff at the institution, or others. In these cases, children may have memories of this fearful, helpless or lonely time in their lives. They might even have scars on their bodies. When they are adopted, these children need to express their feelings about what has happened to them, in order to help them recover from the trauma of the past. The peaceful world in which they are now living is totally different from the world in which they first lived. Even very young children who are not yet able to name what has happened will continue to feel anxious about the period before the adoption.

As parents, you might be inclined to cover up or suppress a history of abuse because you don't want to upset your child unnecessarily. You may be hoping that by not talking about it, your child will eventually forget what happened.

However, talking about abuse is very important to your child. Only by repeatedly dealing with the past in a safe environment will he be able to put these traumatic events behind him and make good progress. It may sound contradictory, but being able to talk about it will give him the best chance of putting the past – and his fears – to rest. Talking will help him to handle overwhelming emotions connected to the first part of his life. If you feel hesitant about this kind of conversation, you could ask for advice from an adoption specialist.

Points to pay attention to and communicate are:

- Your birth parents could not keep you safe, even though they probably wanted to.
- You were not hurt because you were a bad child.
- It wasn't your fault that your birth parents had problems.
- Many people get frustrated or scared if they feel out of control.

If they haven't learnt how to handle their emotions properly, their
first reaction may be to hit other people.
- They hurt you because they didn't know how to cope with their
anger or how to raise a child.
- I could imagine you sometimes feel scared or angry about what has
happened to you. That's normal. I wouldn't find that strange at all.
If you want to tell us anything, or ask a question, even if it sounds
odd, then you need to know that we are always here for you. We
will also understand if you want to cry or be angry.

Concrete information you could tell your child is detailed below.

3–5-year-olds

*Mums and dads must make sure that their children are
safe. Your parents weren't able do that, even though they
probably wanted to.*

Or, if your child was in an orphanage where he was beaten or
treated harshly:

*Your birth mother and father couldn't look after you, so
they took you to a place where they thought the people
would take good care of you until they found a new mum
and dad for you. But these people didn't give you enough
love and attention because they probably had too many
children to look after.*

5–8-year-olds

*You weren't hurt because you were a bad child, even if
someone told you that. I want you to know that it wasn't
your fault at all that you were treated like that. They beat
you because they most probably didn't know how else to
treat a child.*

If your child was treated badly in an orphanage, you could say:

Your nurses were probably so strict because it is very difficult to take care of lots and lots of babies and toddlers who often cry and need a lot of care and attention. Because every day was very busy, they couldn't look after all the children well. Sometimes they got fed up and then they hit the children or tied them up or ignored them because they didn't know what else to do.

If children lived in a very harsh or neglectful orphanage, you could explain why there were so many children there.

8–10-year-olds

Do you sometimes get angry with a friend? So angry that you want to hit him? Many children (and adults) feel that way sometimes, but they have learnt that you can't do that and they cope with their feelings without hitting anyone. Your parents probably never learnt what to do if they felt angry, so they hit you. Deep in their hearts they knew this wasn't right because parents should not hit their children. Maybe your parents were angry because their lives were so difficult. They probably had so many problems that they didn't know what to do. If people get frustrated or scared, they often become angry. At these moments, they often hit you, although it wasn't your fault that they had so many problems.

If your child was mistreated in an orphanage, you could say something similar. In both cases, you could explain that many people (just like children) become frustrated or scared if a situation is not under control. Maybe your child can think of a recent example when he himself was angry, to help him better understand this kind of scenario.

If your child lived in an orphanage, you could say to him:

Babies and toddlers often don't do what adults tell them to do, because they are very little and don't understand. They cry quite a lot, they often fall and they regularly need clean nappies. They also can't eat by themselves. If the nurses have to do all these things for so many children at the same time , they sometimes panic. Then they may hit the children, tie them up or not take good care of them. But all of this didn't happen because you were a naughty child. The nurses were not allowed to hit the children and it doesn't happen in all orphanages. In your orphanage, they didn't know how to cope with the problems properly.

At this age, you could say something about the financial, economic and cultural circumstances of the birth country. This may also partly explain the birth parent's personal circumstances or the situation at the orphanage. It is important that, at this stage, your child gets enough opportunities to feel anger and fear; ask an adoption specialist for help, if you need it.

10–12-year-olds

Try, during this phase, to deal with all your child's memories, both positive and negative. It is important to provide all available information as well as helping your child to cope with his strong emotions about his past. Earlier feelings may also resurface at this age.

Sexual abuse

Some children who have been sexually abused are eventually adopted or placed with a foster family. These children often feel they are to blame for what has happened. The perpetrators frequently convince children that they themselves are to blame; they may make them believe that they share "a secret" or say that they do this because the child is "so special".

Adoptive and foster parents mostly find it very difficult to talk about sexual abuse. They may be shocked by the directness of the words that children use to describe what they have experienced. Parents often try to replace sexual words with less explicit ones, but this is exactly what they should try not to do. The words children choose reflect their feelings about their traumatic experience. If you change the words, children may get the mesage that they have no right to their emotions and that they must think more positively about the abuse. This could result in children refusing to talk about their past.

Often there are only suspicions about whether a child has been sexually abused. Many young children are not able to describe what happened to them; a specialist would have to examine them before a diagnosis could be made, but often sexual abuse will remain unconfirmed. If you suspect abuse, it would be better for you to contact a specialist before talking about it with your child.

If children have memories of abuse, you could talk about it in these ways:

- It was not your fault that you were sexually abused, even though people may have told you it was.
- Your uncle/mother's boyfriend, etc, was only thinking of himself, he was very selfish. He wanted to have a nice feeling and he wasn't thinking of you.
- He touched you in a way that was not good. He is totally responsible for what he did, it was not your fault.

Maybe:

- I think you were very brave to have told your neighbour/teacher/ aunt what he did to you. You did the right thing, you knew what you had to do to be safe.
- Perhaps you feel scared sometimes because of all those confusing things that happened to you.

- If you would like to tell me something about what happened, you can always come to me. I promise you that I will never think what you're saying is bad or funny or stupid. I will always love you, no matter what you feel or think.

It is best to try to create a safe environment so that your child can dare to talk, cry, laugh or shout about his painful memories. In almost every case of sexual abuse, it is best to ask for advice from an adoption specialist.

Concrete information you can give your child is detailed below.

3–5-year-olds

Your birth mother and father couldn't take care of you like other parents. Children need a mum and dad to keep them safe. Your birth parents didn't make sure that you were always safe.

5–8-year-olds

At this stage, you can build on what you said earlier (during ages three–five), but you can also start talking about sexuality. You could read age-appropriate books on this subject together, and you can also give words to what your child has experienced:

I can imagine that you sometimes think about the time you spent with your birth parents. You may feel very angry or sad when you think about it. Maybe you feel scared because so much happened during that time. If you want to talk about your feelings or memories, you can always come to me. I promise I will always believe what you say. I will always love you, no matter what you feel or say.

Reassure your child that nothing he might want to say is too strange or too terrible. Your child must learn that "every feeling is allowed", that not one emotion or memory will change the bond with his adoptive parents. He must learn that by talking about it and by sharing his sadness and anger, he can start to feel better. Your child must also know and believe that you will never send him back, no matter how terrible the things he says are.

8–12-year-olds (and older)

The conversations described above will continue and become more age-appropriate. Before your child reaches adolescence, it might be a good idea to explore the options available for him to have therapy. Maybe he can also attend a peer group where children can talk about their backgrounds and adoption. Of course, it is important to continue to be open and alert to what your child wants to say; and to reassure him that you will always support him.

Rape and incest

If a child was conceived as a result of rape or incest, adoptive parents must be prepared for a very responsible and difficult task – they have to guide their child towards coming to terms with the past. It is essential that you research the psychological problems that these children (and their offenders) have to deal with, perhaps by reading specific literature on this subject or searching for information on the internet. You could also talk to experts on this subject. Children who are conceived as a result of rape or incest usually benefit from one-to-one or family therapy.

It is probably best to contact specialist social workers long before your child is old enough to learn the whole truth. You can then properly prepare yourself for what you need to tell your child and for how to deal with his emotions. He is not only vulnerable because he has been abandoned, but also because of the traumatic circumstances in which he was conceived; by society's rules, he should not have existed.

You may feel more confident if you practise what you need to say with your partner or another person whom you trust so that you can get used to the words. This will also help you to accept the facts, as far as possible. Explaining the facts out loud a couple of times will also make it easier to find the right words. You could also record what you are going to say so that you can hear what your child will hear.

Rape

Concrete information you can give your child is detailed below.

3–8-year-olds

You could begin by making a life story book in which you could refer to the biological father (see Chapter 6). You could start by saying:

We don't know anything about your father.

Adoption therapist Vera Fahlberg says that, in her experience, children only start showing an interest in their birth father from about age eight or nine, because only then do they develop a sense of genetic connectiveness (Fahlberg, quoted in Keefer and Schooler, 2000, p. 110). Susan Pelleq, another US adoption therapist, advises parents to progressively add explanations, such as:

Your mother didn't know your birth father well (or at all). The relationship was not a happy one. Your mother found herself in a situation that was not safe, but something good came of it because you were born.
(Pelleq, quoted in Keefer and Schooler, 2000, p. 110)

8-year-olds and older

Be aware of your child's interest in sexuality from this age. If he understands that it takes two people to create a child, you could say:

Your birth mother and father didn't love each other, they probably didn't even know each other very well. They had sex only because your birth father wanted to. Your mother didn't want to, but she couldn't stop him.

Children fully understand the word "rape" only when they are about 10 or 11 years old. Before that age, you don't need to use the word. It is important that you gradually explain that rape is the result of extreme anger and the need to have total control.

It is better not to delay explanations to spare your child; the "right" time never comes and there is a possibility that he might hear this very painful fact from someone else. If that happens, your child might well feel cut off from you; he would have to cope with the shocking truth all by himself without your support. Your child may then not trust you any more because you did not tell him the truth.

It is not necessary to tell him all the details about the conception. Give your child the same kind of information about sex as you would give to any other child.

Incest

Concrete information you can give your child is detailed below.

3–8-year-olds

You can begin by making a life story book in which the birth father is mentioned (see Chapter 6). You could say that the father was related to the mother. A book about your child's life should only contain the truth and all the facts should initially be stated simply. You can build on information and make it more complex as your child gets older. You should write everything in such a way that your child can easily ask questions at the time and later on.

8-year-olds and older

Children only begin to understand the word "incest" at about age ten or 11, sometimes even later. After offering basic sexual information, you could begin to explain in this way:

Your birth mother is the daughter (or sister, or niece) of your birth father; she became pregnant by him. That should not have been allowed, because a father (brother, uncle) is not allowed to have sex with his own child (sister, niece). Most fathers (brothers, uncles) never do that, but sometimes it happens, if a family has lots of problems and if the father (brother, uncle) doesn't know how he is supposed to love his daughter (sister, niece). This happened to your father and mother, who actually were father and daughter (or brother and sister/uncle and niece). Luckily, something beautiful came out of that relationship and that was you.

Conclusion

If your child was relinquished for very painful or for totally unknown reasons, or if he experienced traumatic events, this places huge demands on you as a parent, especially on your communication skills. You will have to observe your child very carefully and judge when and how he is ready to cope with specific painful facts. You will have to support your child emotionally, and respond to his feelings and thoughts about his past in a sensitive way. Your child will need constant reassurance to give him the confidence to believe that you will stay with him forever and that you will love him no matter what his feelings or thoughts may be.

Most parents do not automatically have these communication skills, which sometimes resemble professional therapeutic skills. It is therefore important to realise that you are not alone in this situation. If you have doubts about what to say and how to say it, or if you are not sure about your child's response to certain information, you should always ask for advice or help from an expert. Sometimes it may be better to tell painful information to your child together with a specialist therapist; you could also discuss a strategy with him/her that you can follow in this regard.

The following chapter discusses communication skills in more detail. Specialised communication skills can help your child to develop basic trust and to feel safer which, in turn, will enable him to express his sadness, fear or shame.

5

Conversation techniques: being sensitive and responsive

A life factor

Adoption is a life factor. Your child will not be preoccupied with it every day, but she will experience her adoptive status as something that keeps coming up in different ways. Brodzinsky uses a striking metaphor to describe this:

> Each of us has things to which we return now and then to work on or worry over – things from the past and present that occasionally resurface and require our attention. It may be the relationship to a sister, it may be a fear of flying, it may be a tragic first love affair or insecurity about our intellectual competence. We tuck these issues away in a hatbox, in a closet, in a far-off corner of the house.

> Every now and then, something makes us search out that far-off corner, open the closet door, take down the box, and deal with the issue for a while. Eventually, we feel finished with it, at least for the time being, so we put away the box and go back to living our lives. Some

day in the future, though, we'll go back to that closet
again, and deal with the issue in the box for a while
longer. That's what the adoption issue is like for most
adoptees – no more, no less.
(1992, p. 22)

If you have adopted children who are already slightly older, this
passage may strike a chord. You will probably have spoken often
together about adoption. In between all the adoption conversations,
your child lives the "rest of her life"; half an hour after a
complicated conversation, she may already be occupied with
something completely different, as if nothing had been said. It is
important to know that this does not mean that most children are
denying their adoptive status. In most cases, they are simply not too
concerned about the subject. Possibly the need for information has
been fulfilled and so life goes on.

This is how it will be throughout their lives. Adopted people will
often be confronted with their past at specific times – on special
occasions, when they get married, have a child, get qualifications.
They are also often faced by their adoptive status if they are
experiencing emotional tension, for example, when their adoptive
parents die.

For all these reasons, the adoption story of your child does not end
when you have passed on all the adoption information. There will
be many milestones and emotional moments that will make your
child think about the facts again and again, and each time a new
conversation about your child's adoption history will begin.

in order to help your child during this life-long process, it is
important that your child develops a basic trust, so that she feels
safe enough with you to express her feelings and thoughts about
her adoption. Children are more able to develop a basic trust if
parents approach them in a sensitive and responsive way. By
carefully listening and observing your child (therefore being
"sensitive") and by responding adequately (therefore being

"responsive"), your child will feel "noticed" and "understood" (Polderman, 1998, pp. 422–433). This two-way process will help her develop a sense of self. In this way she develops a feeling of having a right of existence, an "I-awareness". This in fact means that you have to receive (verbally or non-verbally) your child's initiative or action (Step 1), and then give your own opinion in this regard (Step 2).

Dutch adoption specialist Nelleke Polderman has developed a communication method for adoptive and foster families in which the "naming of behaviour and emotions" is a central theme. This method was derived from Harry Bieman's Video Home Training. In this chapter, I mainly use her step-by-step method (see the appendix at the back of the book) as a basis. According to Nelleke Polderman (2003), adopted children need their parents to have better than "normal" interactive skills, because they have had a difficult start in life and the "normal" principles of interaction between parent and child are often not sufficient. Below, these basic communication methods are explained in more detail.

Naming/identifying behaviour and emotions

Every person, young or old, becomes more self-confident if she is "noticed and understood" by an important person in her environment. Adoption specialists and social workers encourage communication principles that are based on "being noticed and understood". The essential point of these principles is to help parents to "name/identify the behaviour and the emotions of their child". With these interactive principles, parents and children learn to communicate with each other again.

The naming of behaviour and emotions may seem superfluous, but is actually very effective. By doing this, parents are holding a non-judgemental mirror to their child so that she gets the feeling that she is being actively seen and heard. This is the basis for all successful bonding and leads to open communication between parents and children.

Most parents of birth children have a sensitive and responsive approach to their child, an approach that encourages healthy attachment. Adoptive parents must consciously learn to use these interactive principles with their baby, toddler or young child to help them to catch up with what they may have missed out on in the period after their birth.

The naming of behaviour and emotions is essential to help build a basic sense of trust. This requires that you confirm everything that your child does or says. For many parents who start to use this technique, at first it may seem forced, mainly because we usually communicate spontaneously. Learning to communicate more consciously means that parents are forced to say things in a different way. However, it is important to try and persevere with this method, because it can be very helpful when interacting with your child. (This is more fully explained later on in this chapter.) To work effectively, the naming of behaviour and emotions must:

1. be affirmative (therefore not asking a question)
2. be neutral
3. begin with "you"
4. refer to here and now.

Naming/identifying behaviour and emotions with regard to babies and toddlers

Babies and toddlers cannot have a verbal conversation with their parents, but that does not mean that you can't communicate with them through language. Children who are not yet able to express themselves in words develop a basic sense of trust by regularly receiving the message that they have been noticed and understood by you.

Babies and toddlers often respond extremely positively if parents confirm their initiatives or actions, and will develop a secure attachment if parents adequately name their behaviour and emotions, even if they don't yet understand the language.

- Adopted children have often been emotionally and/or physically neglected before they are placed. They can catch up with the feeling of being safe and secure by actively being given attention. Even if adopted children are still trying to adapt to a new environment and don't yet understand the language, the naming of their behaviour and emotions has a positive effect on their development.
- In general, toddlers can be headstrong or moody, but they are not yet able to give words to their bad temper, fear or sadness. When you describe for your child what she feels, does, wants or thinks, she will feel that she is being understood. Often this will make her feel better.

Being sensitive and responsive to your baby or toddler means that you receive the messages your child is giving you by her actions or initiatives, either verbally or non-verbally (Step 1). If you confirm your child's behaviour verbally, you could compare it to having "subtitles" to her initiatives. You could begin with a you-message:

- 'Say what your child is *doing* ('You are drawing with your new pencils')
- Say what your child is *feeling* ('You are very angry now because…')
- Say what your child *wants* ('You want another…')
- Say what your child is *thinking* ('You are naturally thinking…') ' (Polderman, 2003)

You can learn this method step by step. For Step 1, begin, for example, by only naming your child's behaviour or emotions in a simple (affirmative, non-questioning, neutral) way:

You are building a tower.

You are putting another brick on the top. That will become a tower.

You ate all your food.

You took the last bite. Now it's all gone.

You are sad because you want another biscuit.

You got a fright because the balloon made such a loud noise. Bang!

If there are brothers and sisters, you can "complete the circle" by including the brother or sister in the conversation, so that the other child also feels noticed:

Look, Aaron, your brother is drawing something.

Did you see that, Natasha, your sister tied her own shoelace.

Now move on to Step 2. Here, you are explicitly saying something about your own feelings, and that is important for your child's development and self-confidence. Naming also sounds more natural and less technical by using Step 2.

You are building a tower. I wonder how tall it will be!

You ate up all your food. You did that very quickly!

You are sad. I understand that. Come and sit with me and then you can cry. So much has happened in the last few months. I'll hold you tight.

You got a fright when that lady just picked you up. Luckily I am holding you tight now. Look, Aaron, your brother is drawing something. I think it's very beautiful.

Did you see that, Natasha, your sister is tying her own

> *shoelace. Well done! When you get older, you can learn to do that.*

If you name emotions and do not try to suppress sadness, fear or anger, most babies and toddlers will learn to trust because they get the feeling that their parents understand them. Your child's emotions may also eventually subside if you give words to them in Step 1. However, when a child has an angry emotion it is important that you also name/identify the reason for the anger because her anger otherwise may become more intense. If you don't know what the reason is, you can guess. Because you know your child well, there is a good chance you will guess right; if your toddler is angry about something else, she will soon let you know:

> *You are angry, Michelle. You wanted to shower with your sister because we do that every evening.*

If your child confirms that this is the reason why she is angry, you can continue with Step 2. You can show that you understand your child, but that the situation is the way you want it to be at the moment, and that it is not going to change:

> *I understand that you would prefer that. But your sister is sick and is in bed, so tonight you must shower alone.*

You could then guide your child by "positive prompting" – by telling her "what can happen now or later" rather than emphasising "what can't happen now":

> *When Sara is better, you can shower together again.*

Another example of the two-step approach to giving the child a positive view of the future is:

> *You are angry because you don't want to go to bed. I understand that; you want to go on playing with your new toys. However, it is time to go to bed. Take some*

> *toys with you and we will put them in your room so that you can play with them again as soon as you wake up.*

If your child feels noticed and understood, it will be easier for her to accept that the situation is the way it is. You should try and give a positive view of the way the future will be.

In order to make the dialogue "reciprocal", it is important that you use words not only to describe your child's behaviour and emotions but that you also name your own behaviour and emotions. For toddlers, say what you intend to do a few minutes before you do it.

> *I would like to go home soon, Carola. You can play a little longer and then we will get on the bike and go home, so that you can sleep this afternoon.*

> *You want to carry on playing, because it's a lot of fun. However, we are going home in 15 minutes because I need to buy some groceries. After that, you need to sleep.*

This anticipation can help your child focus attention on somebody else till they get ready to comply. Also, it helps your child to predict your behaviour. Predictable behaviour gives children clarity and therefore security – they are not confronted with unexpected, accomplished facts and are therefore better able to accept certain personal behaviour.

If it seems your child is still insecurely attached, it may be best to start by only naming behaviour or actions – giving words to feelings can be too threatening for these children. For instance, name/identify what your child is looking at, or what she is doing with her hands (Step 1) and then comment (Step 2):

> *You are looking outside. I wonder what you are looking at?*

> *You are pointing at the television. I think you want to watch a video.*

> *You are hugging me. I like that very much. It's lovely!*

> *You are shouting very loudly. I think you want another biscuit.*

Naming/identifying behaviour and emotions with young children and those at junior school (children aged 3–10)

Naming the behaviour and emotions (of your child, but also your own) can still be done in an affirmative, neutral way as just described, but as your child's self-confidence grows, it is important that you also give her the space to deny or accept the emotion. If your child responds very strongly to the naming of her emotions, it may be best to name only her behaviour or actions instead, as this will be less threatening to her. From about the age of five or six, you could then go on to talk about your child's sensitive feelings and thoughts. If you give words to what your child does, feels, thinks or wants in a neutral way, you will be able to monitor her reaction:

> *You are playing inside. I have noticed that you play inside a lot lately; before, you used to play outside with Joanna.*

> *You are sad. That's happened quite often in the last few weeks, especially when you come home from school.You are probably thinking: if I help Mum now, then I can go and play outside soon.*

> *You'd rather unwrap the presents now.*

If you suspect why your child is behaving in a certain way, you could suggest:

> *You are possibly sad because you are thinking of your birth mother.*

When your child is angry, it is always best to name/identify the possible reason for it, because anger can become more severe if you only identify the fact that your child is angry:

> *You are angry because you don't want to come grocery shopping. You probably prefer to watch television.*

You may hesitate to make suggestions because you don't want to "take over" your child's feelings or thoughts. However, if your child does feel sad, scared or angry for the reasons that you have suggested, she will feel noticed and understood by you; if she feels that way for another reason, she will say so. She will probably also tell you what is actually going on. An adoptive mother describes what it was like to use this technique with her six-year-old son:

> For the first week I thought I would never learn to name my son's behaviour and emotions properly and that I was getting it completely wrong. But I noticed very soon that it was having a good effect on Jesse. Now that I pay more attention to his feelings, they are really not as invisible as they seemed. If he reacts angrily, I now understand that he is actually sad about something, but that he is not aware of his own feelings. I have learnt to give words to those feelings, and I now say: 'You are shouting at everyone. Maybe you are upset because you can't go to Simon's birthday party.' He often goes on shouting, but then he comes to me and cries his heart out. At these moments, I name his sadness and he knows now that I understand and accept his feelings.

> In the beginning I was always scared that I wouldn't get it right, that I wouldn't name his feelings correctly. But I have noticed that it isn't a problem. He tells me straight away, or I can see it in his face if I have not got it quite right. But I don't say the wrong thing very often. Usually, I simply know what my child is preoccupied with at that moment.

If you name/identify your child's emotions correctly, you will mostly see this in her face. She will feel more relaxed, for example, become less uptight, or she will nod her head or shout out "Yes!".

If you are not sure about a specific feeling, you could choose only to name your child's behaviour (Step 1). You can then give your opinion about it (Step 2):

> *You don't look well. I can imagine that you are not feeling well.*

> *You look so pale and you are so quiet. I am interested in what happened at school.*

Make sure that your child explicitly knows that you understand her behaviour, feelings, thoughts and wishes (even though you can't make her wishes come true).

Here are a few examples of naming behaviour or emotions while at the same time making suggestions about her feelings or thoughts:

> *I see little lights in your eyes. You probably had a nice day at school.*

> *You are so quiet. Perhaps you are thinking about what we spoke of.*

> *You are very happy when we talk about your birthday. It is already eight years since you were born. I often*

think about your birth mother when it's your birthday.
She probably thinks about you on such a special day.
Perhaps you are curious about her and about how she
looks.

Actively receiving what your child says

Active receipt of what your child says will also have a positive effect on the communication, and on her behaviour, as it will ensure that your child feels heard. You can receive your child's words in two ways:

- with body language and voice tone (receipt without words)
- by listening attentively to the words your child uses and then (partially) repeating these words or summarising what she has said (receipt with words, or giving confirmation of receipt).

Receipt without words

Because babies cannot speak, parents automatically use expressive, non-verbal ways to actively receive what their child is communicating. However, it is also important that parents non-verbally receive what older children say.

Examples of non-verbal language are:

- facial expressions
- making eye contact
- using gestures when you speak to your child
- the tone of your voice (warmth of the sound and variations in the tone)– you can "embrace" your child with your voice
- the physical level at which you are communicating, for example, standing up or on your knees
- the attention you give your child by nodding, picking her up, hugging, putting her on your lap, stroking her head or kissing the

sore spot. You actually "name" her pain by giving an attentive kiss (non-verbal) which shows her that you have '"seen" the sore spot. In a magical way, a kiss often seems to stop the pain.

By your non-verbal body language your child will see that she has your attention. This will assure her that she is being heard, and this is especially important to adopted children. Because your child knows that she has been heard, she will feel more safe and develop more basic trust and self-awareness, and, in turn, communicate more openly.

If you would like to get some insight into your own non-verbal behaviour, you could make a video or audiotape of a daily situation where you are communicating with your child. You may already have videos of your family – often just re-playing them and watching yourself and listening to your own voice is enough to make you aware of your body language, your tone of voice and how they might be received by your child.

Receipt with words/giving a confirmation of receipt: repeating and summarising

If your child tells you something, you can respond by literally repeating or summarising what you have heard, so that your child actually hears an echo of her own words.

In fact, you do the same when you name/identify behaviour or emotions: by verbally providing confirmation (Step 1), you hold a non-judgemental "mirror" to her to let her know that she is being heard. With toddlers, who cannot yet speak properly, you could verbalise the sentence that your child probably would want to say. If, for example, she says:

From Dad!

You could give her a confirmation of receipt by saying:

> *This (spoon) is Dad's!*
> *(Polderman, 1998)*

With this confirmation of receipt, you explicitly emphasise what she has just said; if you do this consistently, most toddlers (as well as older children) will get the feeling that they have been heard. With young children, you can repeat what they have said, even if it is unclear, or what they did not finish saying; by doing so, you will make them feel that you are listening to them and will also help positively influence the development of their language.

With older children, you can repeat what they have said by using slightly different words:

Child:

> *I am not going to Granny tomorrow.*

Parent:

> *You don't want to go to Granny tomorrow. You want to stay at home.*

Afterwards (Step 2), you can interpret your child's words and give your own opinion:

> *I don't know if that is practical because both Dad and Mum must work tomorrow and you can't stay home alone. I would like to talk about it again this evening.*

By repeating or summarising what has been said, you give your child an adequate confirmation of receipt. Because your child knows she is heard by you, she will then be better able to hear what you have to say. You can use this repetitive technique to keep a dialogue going. It is then, at the same time, also a method of questioning.

Asking questions

Types of questions

You can have dialogue with your child in two different ways – you can make a neutral, affirmative comment, or ask a direct question. Affirmative sentences end with a full stop, and they have a firm tone, but they often have the impact of a question. Direct questions end with a question mark – they have a querying tone. It is important for parents of adoptees to know the difference between these two ways of responding, because they can have a different effect on the child.

Neutral, affirmative sentences

Neutral, affirmative sentences can imply direct questions, but by using a neutral tone, can make them sound less threatening. The child does not get the feeling that she has to answer you, so she won't clam up too quickly and will be less inclined to give you the answer she thinks you want to hear, instead of what she really feels.

If your child does not talk easily, or she is going through a sensitive period, it is better to put questions into neutral, affirmative sentences. You can do this in the following ways:

- You verbally confirm ("name/identify") your child's non-verbal behaviour or feelings, wishes or thoughts: 'You shrug your shoulders', 'You are so quiet', 'You sound a little down.'
- You confirm your child's words by repeating or summarising what she has said: 'You said that you look strange in the photos', or 'You would rather have stayed in Thailand.'
- You can guess your child's emotions in a neutral way: 'You are perhaps sad because you are thinking about your birth mother', 'You are teased because you look different.'

By ending sentences with a full stop and no question mark, you create a calm, neutral atmosphere. You can carry on talking and maybe even pass on new adoption information without her feeling that she must respond to it.

Direct questions

Direct questions can make your child feel as if she must answer. This may influence the spontaneity and honesty of the answer. However, this does not mean that you can never ask your child a direct question.

How your child reacts depends on her temperament and on her emotional state. An extrovert child will often have less of a problem answering questions than a more withdrawn child. Her willingness to answer freely may also depend on her emotional stability at that moment. She may, for example, be more vulnerable when she is grieving about her past – at these times, direct questions may come across as more threatening.

You can ask a direct question in two ways – as a closed or an open question. You can vary the type of questions, depending on the purpose.

Open questions

These are questions that give your child the freedom to answer as she likes. Your child can determine how much she wants to tell and how long her answer will be. You can ask open questions if you want to gain insight into a specific emotion, thought or fantasy. Open questions often start with "How" or "What". A "Why" question may often come across as a demand for justification. Open questions can be complex for children, and are better used only when you have absolutely no idea what the answer might be.

How do you feel?

What do you think your birth mother looks like?

What do you mean exactly by "sad"?

What can we do about this?

Open questions can be effective if you don't know what your child's feelings are about a particular subject. She may tell you a lot and give you a better understanding of her inner world. You can continue the conversation by asking her about specific points in her answer.

You can also make open questions quite general. This type of question can be effective if you want to talk about a sensitive subject. If you think that your child is being teased at school, for example, and that she prefers not to talk about it, you can begin with an open, general question like:

What do you think of teasing?

Who are the bullies at your school?

Does it sometimes happen to you?

How do you feel if you have been teased?
(Delfos, 2002, p. 119)

Closed questions

These are questions which your child can answer with very few words, mostly "yes" or "no". This generally limits the dialogue. However, asking a closed question can be very effective when you start a conversation or when you want to move it in a specific direction. You can use closed questions if open questions are too broad, if the subject is too sensitive, or if your child isn't a real talker.

A conversation can begin with a few closed questions, and then open out:

Do you like it at school?

What do you like the most?

Are there things you don't like very much?

What are some of the things that you don't like?

Or:

Do you sometimes think about your birth mother?

Do you become sad if you think of her?

Do you fantasise or make up stories about her?

Can you tell me about the mother in your stories and what kinds of things she does?

Asking questions by naming/identifying non-verbal behaviour and emotions

Children are not usually open about or aware of their feelings, especially if they are not yet capable of naming them. However, all children, and many adults, show how they feel by their behaviour. If you learn to read the signals, it will make it easier for you to ask questions.

Children show you what they can't tell you in words: they shrug their shoulders, stare at the ground, fidget with their fingers, fiddle with their hair or bite their nails, don't look at their parents, stay in their room all afternoon, look startled when the word adoption is used, do anything to avoid a conversation, say that 'nothing is the matter', but reveal by their behaviour or their tone of voice that there is something the matter. Also, a poor school report, stomach aches or skin irritations could be non-verbal signals that indicate that your child is not feeling happy.

You can start a dialogue by naming/identifying your child's non-verbal behaviour, emotions feelings, wishes, thoughts, and so on.

> *You don't look at me.*

(You are asking indirectly: 'Do you feel uneasy?')

> *You shrugged your shoulders.*

(You are asking indirectly: 'Aren't you interested in this?')

> *You look sad/miserable.*

(You are asking indirectly: 'What is the matter with you? Why are you so quiet?')

> *You don't seem very happy to me.*

(You are asking indirectly: 'Why have you been reacting so angrily lately?')

It is generally not necessary to ask the direct questions following the statements. Children will respond if you name their non-verbal behaviour or emotion in an affirmative, neutral way. They will not feel interrogated, but rather, heard and understood, and will therefore give you an answer.

Sometimes children say one thing, but then behave in the opposite way. Their behaviour and tone of voice mostly mean more than their words; you can ask questions by naming the contradictions in their message:

> *You say you like the present, but you don't sound very happy about it.*
> *I am not happy.*

You are not happy because you don't think the present is nice.
No, it's because of something else.

So the present is not the reason. What is it then?
Child shrugs her shoulders.

You are shrugging your shoulders. (Don't you want to talk about it?)
I don't know.

You aren't sure.
Today is my birthday.

Yes, today is your birthday. You think that is a reason not to talk about it.
Child walks away, sits at the table and starts drawing.

You've started drawing now. You don't have to talk about it if you don't want to. I want you to know that I understand if you are not happy on your birthday. You can't feel happy unless you are happy. If you want to talk, you can always come to me, even if it is at a strange or unexpected moment, for example, on your birthday.

The conversation could very well end here. The parent has indicated that the emotion has been seen/heard and the "shrugged shoulders" have been noticed. The parent has shown the child that she respects her feelings and the fact that she does not want to talk about it now; she has also offered the child the chance to talk about it at a later stage.

Sentences like:

You look a little miserable.

> *You dropped onto the couch with a big sigh. You have*
> *probably had a difficult day.*

can have the same effect as questions. Your child feels noticed and
will most probably share her feelings with you either fully or partly.

Asking questions by confirming receipt (repeating, summarising)

If you want to start a conversation, you could begin with naming
your child's behaviour and emotions. Your child will respond to this.
You could then give a confirmation of receipt by repeating or
summarising what she has said. This will make her more aware of
what she said, and she may expand on it or explain to you that you
have wrongly interpreted her words. Repeating or summarising can
have the effect of a question and can stimulate her to go on talking.
If your child says, for example:

> *I am happy that Jake is my brother.*

you could respond by confirming her comment:

> *You like it that Jake is your brother.*

She may then go on:

> *Yes, because Jake was also given up for adoption.*

You could then interpret your child's words and ask if your
interpretation is correct:

> *You mean you are glad you have a brother in the same*
> *situation, so that you can talk about it together. (Is that*
> *right?)*
> *Yes!*

By repeating/summarising what your child has said, you indirectly ask questions and continue the dialogue. Be careful not to use this technique too often, because constantly repeating what your child has said can also irritate her, especially when she is a little older. Try to alternate between confirming what you heard, and giving your own opinion or asking a direct question:

> **You don't wear your red shoes any more.**
> *No.*
>
> **Don't they feel comfortable?**
> *Yes, they do. I don't really like them.*
>
> **You don't like them. That's a pity.**
> *They are stupid.*
>
> **You think they are stupid. I didn't know that.**
> *Janelle says that they are stupid.*
>
> **Oh! Janelle says that.**
> *Yes, she thinks they are stupid. She thinks I'm stupid.*
>
> **Janelle thinks you are stupid. That isn't nice for you.**
> *No, that isn't it. She thinks my nose is funny.*
>
> **Your nose.**
> *Yes. My nose is flat and she thinks that it's ugly.*

Another example:

> **You don't want a beautiful new dress for your birthday.**
> *No. I don't need one.*
>
> **Oh, you don't need one. That's a pity, because I wanted to buy one with you.**
> *I don't need to look nice on my birthday.*

Why don't you need to look nice on your birthday?
(Child shrugs her shoulders.)

You shrug your shoulders. Maybe you don't like having a birthday?
I don't want to celebrate my birthday.

You don't want to celebrate your birthday. I didn't know that. Last year you liked it very much when it was your birthday.
At my birthday I have to pretend I'm happy and I don't feel like doing that.

You could also summarise a longer dialogue. Try to be as objective as possible when you repeat in your own words what you have heard (Step 1). In your summary, you could include something about the emotions that your child expressed, either verbally or non-verbally. In conclusion, you should ask her whether you have got it right.

You would rather not celebrate your adoption day because on this day you always feel sad. It makes you think about the video we took when we held you in our arms for the first time. You were crying because you had to say goodbye to your carer, and you didn't want to leave her. At that moment we were still strangers so you didn't want to come with us. You don't want to have to feel happy on a day that actually makes you very sad. Is that right?
(Child nods)

You can now go on by adding your own opinion or thoughts (Step 2):

I can understand that you don't like to think back to that day; it was a frightening and sad moment for you.

You could then offer an alternative to the adoption day celebration, an alternative that matches your child's feelings:

> *Maybe we shouldn't have a party this year, but instead, we could burn a candle for your carer; perhaps we could write her a letter or draw something for her? What do you think of that?*

Or you could ask your child what she would prefer to do on that day. It is, in any case, important that you don't try to suppress her sadness by offering fun alternatives or by not talking about it further. This could give your child the feeling that you don't approve of her sadness.

Asking questions by responding to subjective words

In almost every sentence, people (unconsciously) give signals about their feelings by using "subjective words". Subjective words are words that are differently interpreted or experienced by different people, for example: I feel contented, lucky, beautiful, ugly, strong, magnificent, angry, sad, strange, crazy. All of these words have a unique emotional connotation for each one of us. Other words that have many different, personal meanings are, for example: terrible, dark, light, nice, pretty, painful, sick, stupid, far, close, soon, earlier, difficult, easy, cold, warm, real, beautiful. We also experience colours subjectively.

If your child says:

> *I think I was ugly when I was a baby.*

You could ask about the word "ugly" to get more insight into your child's experience – she probably understands the word "ugly" in a different way to you:

You think you look ugly in these photos.
What do you mean by ugly?

If your child does not react, you could make a neutral guess:

You think that perhaps you were ugly as a baby because you had so little hair?

The following is an example of a conversation in which you start by naming your child's behaviour and she gives you an answer which includes a subjective word:

You haven't shown any interest in reading books or looking at photos about your adoption recently.
No, I think it is stupid.

You think the photos are stupid.
Yes. I look very strange.

What do you mean by strange?
I think that I have weird eyes.

Why weird?
Joanna has different eyes.

You could go on with naming the factual situation (because you can't change it and you don't need to change it) and by asking how your child feels about the situation in a questioning or affirmative tone:

That's right. Joanna has different, rounder eyes.
Joanna teases me all the time, she says that I have stupid eyes.

Would you like to have the same eyes as Joanna?
Yes. I wish I wasn't adopted because then I would look normal.

You could give your own opinion at this stage, to show that you've heard what she has said:

> *I understand that. You would like to look like all the other children. I feel sad for you that it isn't like that.*

Don't immediately try to turn the dialogue into something positive. You will probably be very tempted to do so because you want your child to feel better about herself. But children (as well as adults) experience a positive response in this kind of situation as a denial of how they really feel. Try to respect your child's feelings. At a later stage, a positive approach might help your child; you could then mention her beautiful looks or her special inner qualities. In this context, you could also bring the birth parents into the conversation by, for example, wondering whether your child looks like them.

Adoptive parents should be alert to specific subjective words relating to adoption. If a child says that she thinks she looks strange in her baby photos, it is important that you not only ask about the subjective word "strange", but that you find out why she thinks she looks strange in the photos. She may think that there was something wrong with her as a baby and that this was the reason why she was put up for adoption:

> *I don't want to see any more baby photos of myself.*
> *Oh, you don't want to see any more baby photos. That's a pity.*

> *I looked stupid when I was a baby.*
> *What is so stupid about you when you were a baby?*

> *I have a weird head.*
> *You think that you had a weird head, so you don't want to see any more photos.*

The back of my head is totally flat and I had no hair.
Yes, that's right. Do you think that your birth mother also
thought that you looked weird?

Child nods.

Maybe.

Have you ever seen photos of other babies? When
children are just born, they always look a little weird.
Their heads still need to become round, and most
babies still need to grow hair. But there isn't one
mother who thinks that her baby looks strange, and I
know for sure that your mother didn't think so either.
She thought you were a beautiful baby, just like we did,
even though she couldn't look after you.

Asking questions by giving choices

Sometimes it is best to offer your child some structure during a
dialogue, especially if she is overwhelmed by her feelings and
doesn't know what she should say. If you think she wants to tell you
something but doesn't know how, you could ask her a closed
question with one or two choices:

Should we go to the zoo on your birthday or should we
do something else?

Are you so sad because you don't like your gift, or is it
because of something else?

How did you get on with Esther today? Did the two of
you play or practise your sums?

What do you think of this solution? Are you happy with it, or shall we work out another way together?

By giving your child clear choices, you will enable her to think more clearly herself: I don't want this but I do want that, or I feel this but I don't feel that. She can determine how she actually feels and what she prefers to do, and this confirms that her wishes are important to you.

General points to consider

- Children can react very differently to your naming of behaviour and emotions. One child will decisively say 'Yes!' or 'No!' if you name/identify her emotions; another child will hardly react at the time, but may, days or weeks later, include it in her play. Most children become more well balanced when parents name their behaviour and feelings.
- Even parents react differently to naming. One parent may react impulsively whereas another may pause for thought. An adoptive mother writes:

> My husband always prefers to react immediately. It takes a lot for him to control his impulsive way of responding and think it through before reacting to our daughter's behaviour. Our daughter is so fast and impulsive, and by the time we have gone through all the steps of naming, she is already on to something else. On days when I am tired, I too find it difficult to stay alert and keep track of things and to name/identify her behaviour and emotions. This communication method is not easy, it is hard work, especially during the first few weeks or even months, and sometimes it still takes a lot of effort now. However, I am very happy that we have carried on with it, because I often see that it is having a positive effect on my child, and that is really wonderful.

- If you want to start a serious conversation, face your child at her level. Try to keep eye contact. Get into your child's inner world – talk, think and move at her level.
- Do not question your child's emotions. Go with her: if she is sad, don't try to cheer her up – she will come out of her sadness when she is ready. It can happen sooner if you name her feelings objectively while she is sad.
- Don't doubt your child's words, even though what she says might sound exaggerated. If appropriate, question her closely about subjective words, because these words may express something important about your child's inner world.
- If your child prefers not to talk, then let it be. Create a future opportunity by saying that she can always come and talk to you if she wants to, and that it isn't a problem that she doesn't want to speak now. Teach your child that she is always allowed to say 'I dont want to talk now.'
- If your child doesn't ask any questions about her adoption and doesn't give any answers, this may not mean that she is not interested. Tell her that you are always prepared to talk about her adoption but that she must never feel she has to.
- You could use the "pebbles technique": pebbles are one-liners, not conversations, that raise an issue and are then allowed to ripple until the child is ready to pick up on it. By "dropping a pebble" about adoption, you may encourage your child to start thinking about a specific topic (van Gulden and Bartels-Rabb, 2001, p. 200). A pebble can be a sentence that says something about genetic relationships or can represent a feeling, the birth mother or the child herself:

> *You play the violin so beautifully. Maybe your birth mother has musical talent. Or maybe you got this talent from your birth father. I often wonder whom you got this talent from.*

The pebbles technique can also refer to something you have heard of or read about:

> *I have heard that adopted children sometimes feel that it was their fault that they were put up for adoption.*

According to van Gulden and Bartels-Rabb, parents must try to ensure that these one-line comments don't become direct questions because then your child will 'try to guess the right answer rather than answer sincerely and risk hurting you or being reprimanded' (2001).

The purpose of the pebbles technique is that your child does not feel obliged to give an answer. She can think it over and come back to it at a later stage if she wants to. By using these one-liners, you are telling your child that it is fine to be curious about her birth parents, or to be sad on her birthday or adoption day, and that she can talk to her parents about her adoption-related feelings and thoughts.

- Be careful not to judge your child in general terms if she does something that is not acceptable to you: she might get the feeling that it is not her behaviour that is being named, but that she is being judged as a person. It is important to try to make the distinction between the child's behaviour and the child herself. Sentences like:

> *You are not nice.*

> *You are being horrible.*

contain judgements about your child, whereas it was only her behaviour that you wanted to name at that moment. Try to remain as neutral as possible; name your child's behaviour in an objective way and then give your opinion on it:

You have been lying on the ground screaming for ten minutes now. I don't like that because it is hurting my ears.

With toddlers and young children, it can help to say:

I love you very much, but I want you to stop screaming now.

6

Ways to talk about adoption

Beginning a conversation

Your child's adoption will be a fact of life. By reacting sensitively and responsively to your child, he will most probably develop more basic trust. As a result, he may feel more safe and therefore be able to express his feelings and any concerns he may have more easily. You could start talking to your child about adoption by reading books that relate to the subject, by looking at photos together, by filing the adoption documents with him (e.g. medical reports, information you received about the birth parents) or by entering into your child's pretend play. This chapter looks at a variety of practical ways of discussing adoption with your child.

Concrete approaches

Show photographs and videos

The easiest way to start talking to toddlers and young children about their adoption is by looking at photographs. If you travelled to adopt your child, you probably have pictures of the birth country, the actual journey and of the moment when you first held him. If your child was handed over to you at the airport, you probably have images of this moment. Some parents also have photos of the foster parents, the orphanage and/or the birth family.

It will depend on the age of your child as to whether you show him these photos soon after arrival, or later. Babies and young toddlers may not recognise the people in the photos or video material. However, you don't need to tell your child everything right away, but you can establish a routine of looking at pictures that tell the story of his adoption. You might also show him the clothes he was wearing when you brought him home. This can make the situation more tangible, even for young toddlers. As your child gets older, you can expand on the basic account of what happened, by showing him more photos of the orphanage, the birth or foster parents, and his birth country. You may also have photographs or a video of his arrival in his new family and new country.

Toddlers and young children, but also slightly older children, often like to have a special album of their favourite pictures that they can look at whenever they want, either alone or with their family or friends. Think carefully about including photos of the birth parents or the orphanage.

Display maps of the world or the birth country

One way of starting a dialogue about the birth country is to show your child a map of his country of origin, or of the world. Toddlers and young children do not know how far away their native country is. It is 'very, very far away', they say, but they generally have no idea what that really means. It's like being told that their birthday is still a long, long time ahead! Toddlers and very young children only really understand "now", "here" and "there". If you hang up a map of the world, the distance between where he lives now and his country of origin will become more real. If you can find a map with nice drawings, you could spend time with your child talking about the world in general.

You could also buy a map of the birth country and mark the area and the city your child comes from. If he is a little older, you could buy a street map of the city and show him exactly where he was found, where his birth parents live and where the orphange is.

Talk about the birth country

To an extent, your child will feel a connection, however intangible, to his birth country; he will feel foreign. By regularly paying attention to the culture and politics of his native country, you will help your child to integrate his two identities. You can do this by celebrating festive days that are related to his country of birth, by listening to music from that country, by regularly cooking local dishes, by adopting typical habits like "eating with sticks" (if, in his birth country, they use chopsticks), by buying clothes in the style of those worn in the birth country, or books about the region.

You could also collect newspaper articles, documentaries or films that say something important about the situation in the birth country. If your child is old enough (approximately aged eight–12), you could consider traveling to his native country, but it is important to find out whether your child really wants to go.

Read stories about adoption

There are a fair number of picture and reading books available in bookshops and libraries that cover the topic of adoption (see *Useful Books*). Adoption agencies sometimes also have an extensive selection of children's books on adoption.

Read about topics related to adoption

Adopted children are often preoccupied with specific subjects related to adoption. They might have a fear of abandonment, experience loyalty conflicts or have a negative self-image. However, these are not problems that only adopted children have. A lot of "normal" children find themselves in situations either at home or at school where they also develop a fear of abandonment, a negative self-image, loyalty conflicts or sadness related to the loss of a special person. Children's books often focus on these topics. These are universal themes, but at the same time touch each individual child's deepest feelings.

It can be very liberating to read these books, especially for adopted children. They can identify with the main character without focusing directly on their own adoptive status. In this way, adopted children can "deal with small chunks at a time" and keep their own sadness about being given up for adoption at a safe distance for a while.

In addition, they may feel liberated because in some respects they seem no different to other children, as other children also experience things in life that make them feel insecure or sad. Friends at school may also be teased because they have red hair or because they have a gay father or an overweight mother. They may also sometimes experience loyalty conflicts or fears of being left alone, for example, if their parents get divorced. They, too, may sometimes dream of "being rescued" from very strict parents or parents who don't seem to care very much about them.

Themes relating to adoption are:

- attachment / basic trust
- being different
- fear of abandonment
- being lost and then found again
- negative self-image
- awareness of ethnic identity
- having secrets or fantasies that you don't dare to tell
- loyalty issues, not being able to choose between Mum or Dad
- feeling sad and not being able to express it
- being aggressive or angry and not really understanding why

- feeling that nobody knows who you really are
- fantasies about having a different dad or mum who are much nicer than your own
- wanting to be rescued
- feeling homesick
- having a sense of loss; grieving.

Give an adoption content to festive days

On festive days, people often celebrate a happy, joyful event or meeting they remember as important from the past. Adopted children are confronted by their adoption on these occasions, either willingly or unwillingly. It may happen on their own birthday, on the anniversary of their adoption, on Mother's Day, Father's Day, but also on days when your child has graduated, or reached some other milestone, at Christmas or New Year. Celebratory days may bring good feelings, but may also cause anger and sadness. Slightly older children often will not only be reminded of the family event that is being celebrated, but also of how their birth parents rejected them; they may feel sad about the people who are absent.

If you can be open to your child's emotions on these special days, he may feel safe enough to express his sadness or anger. Below are a few tips to help you to handle your child's feelings.

- Ask your child how he is feeling on this day: is he looking foward to the party, or is he perhaps sad or angry, or is he thinking of his birth parents? You could write a letter together or make a drawing (see later sections on writing letters and drawing pictures).
- Create a ritual by burning a candle for his birth mother and by wishing her all the happiness in the world.
- Talk about the day that he was born (if you know something about this day) and about how happy his birth parents most probably were with him being born, even though they had to give him up for adoption.
- Play a favourite CD. Children are often sensitive to pop songs with a

text they can relate to. Your child might like to hear music from his birth country.

If your child is able to express his sadness before the celebrations, he might be able to enjoy himself a few hours later, but it is important that you allow him to remain sad or angry for the whole day, if he feels the need to.

Maintain contact with other adoptive families

Many parents travel overseas to adopt their child. Sometimes, they travel in a group with other adopters. The children adopted by such "travel groups" often have a social bond: they come from the same orphanage or the same area, they have possibly slept next to each other, were born in the same region or were adopted on the same day. Any of the parents in a group could, in principle, have become their parents. Many families organise reunions, to meet each other and to see how the children are growing up and developing, but these reunions often stop after a few years, as adoptive parents often have less need to stay in contact when their children are settled. Some may have already returned for a second or third time to adopt another child.

However, it is still important for the parents, as well as the children, to stay in contact with other adoptive families. Parents can share experiences. Children from the age of approximately eight can support each other and talk to each other about their lives at school and at home, about their adoption-related grief and their happiness – they will know that they are not alone, and that there are other children who look like them and share similar experiences. A few children feel "related" for life to one or more children from their travel group.

If you were not part of a travel group, you can maintain contact with families you met during preparation classes or other events organised by your adoption agency. Even children who do not come from the same region or who come from a different country are able to support each other.

Maintain contact with or offer help to those remaining in the birth country

Always be alert to your child's "conscience questions" relating to the social and political situation in his birth country. Consider being actively involved from the beginning with the birth or foster parents, the orphanage, or more generally with the under-privileged children in the birth country. Your child might feel that he is contributing something concrete to the welfare of those who stayed behind if you send drawings or photographs to the foster or birth parents every year, or if you buy toys and clothes for the children at the orphanage together. Maybe you could collect gifts from your travel group each year. If you are actively involved, your child will see that you are doing your best to help children who were left behind and that you have a genuine interest in his birth country. Keeping in touch with the birth country also creates good opportunities to talk to your child about his adoption.

Documentary approaches

Make a memory box

You can keep all kinds of things in a memory box that your child is then able to look at whenever he likes, either alone or with you. He may choose a special box himself if he is old enough to do so. Mementoes you could keep are: the adoption application and order, birth certificate, medical information, city road map, photographs of the orphanage and of the birth or foster parents, a baby "footprint", baby photographs, photographs of his birth city and a map showing where he was born, a stone from the place he comes from (you could make a necklace or a ring with it later on) or soil from where he was born, the clothes that he wore when he was given to you, the passport and his visa to enter his new country, the

plane ticket home, the residence permit and any other official
adoption documents. Translations should be stored in the box, so
that your child can read the papers himself when he is old enough.

The memory box can fulfil a very important function for your child.
Femmie Juffer writes:

> Not only are his background and his past encapsulated
> in the box, but also the adoption documentation, and
> therefore his present and future. By having insight, for
> example, into the official adoption decision, your child
> will understand that important people, even a judge,
> have acknowledged that the adoptive parents have
> become his new parents.
> (1999, pp. 107–108)

Femmie Juffer advises parents to ensure that their child (when he is
old enough) always knows where the adoption papers can be found
so that he can look at them whenever he feels the need to do so.

Create a baby book

In a baby book, you can record all the important moments in your
child's life. You could start with diary entries about the time you
were waiting before travelling to meet your child. You could include
photographs of the nursery where he lived, messages of
congratulations that you and your child received, photographs of
the arrival at the airport, of his first birthday in his new country and
of the formal adoption hearing. Later, you can choose what else to
record or stick in the book: perhaps a lock of baby hair, the first visit
to a playgroup, the first photograph of your child with his new
brother or sister, the day he started school, the day he got his
swimming certificate, and so on.

Create a family book

If you have a family that includes birth children as well as adopted children, you could consider making a family book (Juffer, 1999, p. 127). The differences and similarities between the siblings are then obvious and open to discussion. It is best to begin with the period before you had children. Then you can show how each child joined the family, for example, by sticking in photographs of pregnancy and birth, and of the journey to the country where you adopted your other child(ren). You could illustrate the specific cultural differences between the birth countries of all your children. You can involve your children in making the book by drawing pictures or choosing photos or images from magazines to cut out and stick in.

Write an adoption story book

You can read books about adoption with your child, but you can also write your own. You can do this in two ways.

A story book written from the parent's perspective

In a storybook you can tell your child who you are and why you adopted him. Preferably, put one simple sentence on each page, and write it in the third person: 'There was a woman called Anna and a man called David.' This lends the story a certain distance, and might make it easier for your child to ask questions. Illustrate each page with a drawing or a photo. An example of an adoption story might be:

> Say who David and Anna were, what they liked to do most and how much they loved each other. Explain how much they wanted a child (and add if appropriate that they couldn't have/make children of their own) and that they then decided to write a letter to an adoption agency. In the letter they asked: If you know people

who can't take care of their child, will you please let them know that we would really like to be that child's parents? Tell how long Anna and David needed to wait and that it was difficult having to wait so long because they really wanted to care for a child. Explain in very simple words that there is an agreement in the world that parents who want to adopt someone else's child must first get a kind of certificate; this means birth mothers and fathers can be sure that their children will get a good mum and dad.

Describe how Anna and David eventually got their certificate after waiting a very long time, and that they were then allowed to become a mum and dad. Explain that they finally got a phone call from the adoption agency to say that a lovely mother had given birth to a child but that she could not take care of him. Anna and David then saw a photo of the baby. It was a boy and his name was Carlos.

Write how happy Anna and David were when they heard his beautiful name and saw how cute he looked. Say how sad the birth mother was when they came to adopt the baby but also that she very much wanted to make sure that her child had a safe home. Also say that baby Carlos was a bit sad in the beginning, but that he now had a mum and dad who were able to give him a loving family. When he came home with his new parents, there was a party with lots of balloons. WELCOME HOME, CARLOS! was on the door in big letters.

A story book written from the child's perspective

In this story book, you can tell a story through the eyes of your child: where he comes from, why he was adopted and what it means to be adopted. In this book your child can show who he is.

An adoptive mother describes how she and her five-year-old daughter made a book:

> When Jennifer was five years old, I made a book with her about how she came into our family. We put drawings in it, and wrote very simple sentences and chose meaningful photographs. I used an A5 ring-binder with plastic sleeves, so she could easily slide the pieces of paper in and out. She has just turned six, but she still often looks at the book and wants me to read it to her. She knows several pages off by heart and pretends to read them herself. A few weeks ago she took the book with her to show it to her new teacher. I explained to the teacher what kind of book it was. He read it out aloud to the children in his group. Jennifer showed the photographs and enjoyed sharing the story with her class.

Make an adoption life story book

In an adoption life story book, you describe and illustrate the period from birth to the adoption, together with your child. Beth O'Malley has written very good books on this subject and in her book, *Lifebooks*, gives many examples (2002). As an adoption expert, she has a lot of experience with creating adoption life story books.*

According to O'Malley, an adoption life story book should include everything that happened from the moment the child was born to the moment he was officially adopted. You should mention all the facts (at your child's level of understanding) of this first period in his life. The book should be about the day of birth, the birth parents, the foster family, the orphanage, the reason why your child was

*O'Malley uses European terminology, which refers to such books as adoption life books. In UK terminology, they are commonly called adoption life story books and we have used this term here.

given up for adoption, the birth country and the biological brothers and sisters (if present). You should record this in colourful pages and in short, simple sentences. According to O' Malley, you should put at least one graphic or photo on each page (2002, p. 39). If you don't know certain facts, you could together creatively add fantasy drawings, short letters and poems. The book should be attractive and there must be humour in it, otherwise your child will not have the focus to read or work in it on a regular basis.

In *Lifebooks*, O'Malley indicates all the details that, in any case, should be included:

- a title page with a photo of your child or a self-portrait by your child
- a birthday page and, if you know it, the exact time of birth
- a birth page, with the meaning of the child's name, and all known facts about the birth
- a copy of the birth certificate
- a "where did I come from" page, describing the birth mother and the growing-in-her-tummy story
- a "facts of life" page about the "birds and the bees" (where do children come from – here you can also mention the birth father)
- a birth parents' page with drawings that your child can add to as his understanding develops over the years. If you have no information about the birth parents, you should write down that the details are unknown.You could fantasise together about what they are doing now, what they might look like, which talents or characteristics your child has probably inherited from them, and so on
- a birth country page with information and pictures about the language, celebrations and festivals, food, photos of people who look similar to your child
- a "why was I adopted" page with a simple explanation, with space for more complex information to be added when your child is older
- pages with details of the adoption agency, the social workers and the judge who were involved in the adoption (this helps the child understand that he wasn't "taken" or "kidnapped" and that the birth mother wasn't coerced)
- an orphanage or foster carer page with information about where

your child lived before the adoption took place
- a "joining our family" page with festive stories and pictures about the day your child joined you
- a "question" page with space for your child to write down what still puzzles him, for instance, 'Why did my brothers stay in Brazil?'

A life story book can grow with your child as he grows older; extra pages or chapters can always be added. You could also put in letters or photos that he has received from his foster or birth parents; words or symbols from his country of birth can be drawn or stuck onto a page as well as cuttings from magazines with scenery from the birth country or pictures of the people who live there. Recipes and pictures of favourite food that originates from the birth country can also be pasted in.

A life story book can have therapeutic value – if your child goes through a period when he is preoccupied with his adoption, you can read the life story book together. Sometimes, he will feel the need to leaf through the book with you and to talk about it. At other times, he might prefer to write or draw something to add to the book.

If your child is still very young, you can fill in some details yourself. On some pages you could write down simple, short sentences. It gives you the chance to get used to the story that you need to tell your child. First, write your short sentences down on a piece of scrap paper. Sleep on it a few nights and say the words out loud a few times. Ask you partner what he or she thinks about how the words sound. Are they suitable for your child to hear? Did you unconsciously add in truths in a subjective way that your child might ask about and to which you can't provide an answer?

As your child grows older, you could create pages on new topics together. Always look for pictures together with your child.

Be aware that a life story book does not have to look "nice and beautiful": it is a "work book" for you and your child to use. Make good-quality photocopies of all the pages and use these instead of the originals. Your child can then use this life story book in the way it was intended; he doesn't need to be extra careful and in case it is lost or damaged, you can always make a new copy. If you can, use acid-free paper for the originals, so that the book and drawings will last a long time (see *Useful Books* for titles on life story work).

Imaginative approaches

Writing letters

Perhaps your child would rather write a letter to his birth parents than talk about them. Words acquire a deeper meaning when they are written down, even if the other person isn't always able to read them.

Some people feel the urge to write a letter to someone they loved who has died. Children can feel a similar urge about a lost parent (aunt, friend, brother, grandmother). They may want to attach a letter to a balloon and let it float into the sky, or put a message in a bottle and throw it in the sea. They may write messages that they would not say out loud to their lost relative or friend. The fact that this letter will never be read is not important, although children might fantasise that a balloon has reached the lost loved one.

Mostly, adopted children have living parents whom they are not able to reach. On special days, or at difficult moments, you could ask your child whether he would like to write a letter. You could ask: 'If you wrote your birth mother a letter, what would you put in it?' or say: 'I could imagine that you would want to send your birth mother a letter.' If he wants to, you could read the letter together and talk about it. You might start an annual ritual of writing a letter on a symbolic day. Your child could keep these letters in his memory box or in his life story book. Letters do not need to be long – one line can be enough, if your child simply wants to say that he misses his birth father or mother, that he hopes that they are happy, and that he himself is happy.

Drawing pictures

What applies to letters also applies to drawings – drawings can also express feelings about adoption. Ask your child how he imagines his birth parents and the environment in which he thinks they live. If he wants to, let him draw a picture and talk about what he has drawn. You don't need to interpret the drawings, but rather just name/identify what you see. You will be able to start a conversation about it anyway.

If you want to talk about other feelings relating to the adoption, you may do this too by visualising images/feelings. Drawings often give insight into your child's feelings. You could ask him, for example, to create a beautiful flower, a fairy-tale tree, an ideal birthday, his favourite present, his dream for the future, etc. Take part yourself. Both of you could draw a beautiful flower on a piece of paper and then compare them. What does your child's flower look like? Does it have lots of colour? Is it a thin, frail flower, swaying dreamily or searchingly in the air, or is it a strong, well-rooted flower? What shape does the flower have? Is it a thin stripe, a shooting rocket, or is it outlined by a warm, round sun? You could stimulate a dialogue by telling him what you see: the form of the face, his use of colour, the symbols that he has drawn. You could also encourage your child by asking him, while he is drawing, what he means or feels about certain figures or colours. Be careful not to incorporate too many of your own emotions or thoughts. Drawings will give your child the chance to express his own feelings. If you are disturbed or worried about your child's colours or images, you can ask for advice from an adoption expert.

Naturally, you can also think of other ways to visualise your child's feelings or fantasies. He could, for example, create a collage, mould some clay or play with sand, etc. Identifying/naming what you see is actually sufficient. Children often unconsciously continue to think about these visualised feelings.

You may do the same with his drawings as you do with his letters: store them in the life story book or in the memory box, or let them fly into the air attached to a balloon. You could also frame them and give them a special place in your home.

Making use of play

Children often express themselves in play: they make up stories with dolls or animals; they dig holes in the sand, lay foundations and build a castle; they dress up, dance, race cars and fight with toy weapons; or pretend to be teachers, doctors and nurses. In this way, children reveal their concerns and preoccupations. In fact, children's play can be compared with dreaming: both are based on elements of reality. However, underneath this reality, emotions are symbolically expressed.

The function of play is threefold.

1. By allowing your child to initiate play, you enable him to handle his emotions. You best identify/name your child's spontaneous play (behaviour, emotions) in an affirmative and neutral way (Step 1) to give your child more "I-awareness". By doing this, your child also possibly becomes still more concentrated during his play and therefore may be able to work through his emotions even better. While your child initiates play, it is not necessary to give your opinion or to ask for a response (Step 2), for example, you don't need to ask whether your child heard you. If you do give your opinion, it is important that you closely mirror your child's play ('That seems to be nice for the monkey' or 'I guess that hurts very much', and so on). This can help your child continue with his play.

2. By entering into your child's play, you can get an insight into his feelings and his level of understanding about his concerns and feelings.

3. You may reduce fears or other emotions that your child expresses while playing by suggesting "a good ending", or, if your child is a little older, you could talk later about the expressed emotions and connect them to reality.

If you are able to enter and share your child's play by naming what you see and by taking on the role of a doll or an animal, you can help your child come to terms with his emotions and, at the same time, get to know more about what he feels.

However, this is different to using *play therapy*. Initiating complex, symbolic play should not be done without a professional counsellor who can help you interpret what is happening. Try never to take your child's feelings personally. If intense loss is expressed in play, identify and name your child's feeling or behaviour, and then ask for advice from an adoption specialist.

Toddlers are especially good at showing their thoughts and feelings through play. If they feel safe, they begin with pretend-play at a very young age. If they have just got a new baby sister or brother, they may start pretending that they are also a little baby. Sometimes they want to suck on a dummy again, to drink out of a baby bottle or even to wear a nappy. They are unconciously compensating for what they are missing. As a parent, you can participate in this pretend-play very easily.

Toddlers and young children enjoy playing with dolls, animals or soldiers and making up stories that are related to attachment and separation, aggression and control, care, love and "nurturance" (Watkins and Fisher, 1993, p. 64). Through play, toddlers can unconsciously give a safe meaning to some adoption-related issues. Themes relating to adoption include:

- losing his way, hiding and being found
- doing scary or dangerous things and being rescued by Mum or Dad
- running away from home and then coming back

- carrying a baby in the tummy and giving birth to it
- hugging and caring for a baby doll (and maybe, when the child gets a bit older, throwing the baby away, hitting it or breaking it)
- being angry, destructive or being sent away and then being hugged again
- being alone and then together again
- making a safe area to be in, like a tent, a canopy hanging over the bed, a hut or cave, or a sleeping bag.

Just by a simple hide-and-seek game and by expanding on it a little, parents can make toddlers feel safe. Play may alleviate the fear of separation, or at least make it more manageable for your child.

The following is an example from an adoptive mother of a five-year-old boy who suddenly started a pretend game which was related to the fact that he was found.

> Ricardo fetched a blanket, put it on the ground and asked his father: 'Would you please wrap me up properly, Dad?' Harry (his father) wrapped him up tightly and warmly. Ricardo gave a few more instructions and when he was finally properly "wrapped up", he called for me as well. 'Now you must find me and then you're very happy,' he said, 'but at first, you don't see me.' We walked around a little and asked where he was lying. 'On a deserted road in the forest,' came the reply. We walked around him some more and pretended that we didn't see him. Then he started to cry softly. Harry knelt down and found the child in the blanket. 'Oh, Mum, come and look here,' he said, 'there is a nice, little baby wrapped up in a very warm blanket.' I also knelt down. 'Oh,' I said, 'what a beautiful, sweet baby!' Ricardo said that we must take him out of the blanket. Harry started to unravel the blanket and when he was eventually unwrapped and lying on the blanket, I again said: 'Oh, what a sweet, beautiful child! It is a boy, Dad, a very nice little boy!'

Ricardo said that we were allowed to pick him up and take him with us. 'Can I really do that?' I asked. 'May we take this amazing little boy home and look after him?' Ricardo nodded. Harry picked him up and we both looked at our son. 'We can look after him, isn't that great? I am happy! I have never been so happy!' I said loudly. 'I have never seen such a beautiful child, Mum', Harry said. 'We are going to look after him forever and he will live with us forever. Even if he cries or is angry, we will always love this special little boy.'

When the game was finished, Ricardo looked very contented. He was feeling safer, wanted more hugs and was more aware of himself. Thereafter, he asked to play the same game almost every day and he always wanted it to be the same. He gained a lot of self-confidence through it . After a few months, he asked for it less and less often. He is now six years old and still wants to play the game now and again; he asks to be wrapped up in the blanket again, and with all our love, we do it.

Another adoptive mother told me that her seven-year-old daughter Maya wasn't much of a "talker", and during the past few weeks she had been very moody.

One day, Maya was playing with some dolls. I came to sit near her and asked her what she was playing. 'Mummy,' she said, 'do you also want to play with me?' I nodded. 'What do you want me to do?' Maya fetched a doll and gave it to me. 'You are baby Eric's mother. Eric is your real son and you are going to hug him.' 'Is this Eric?' I asked. 'Yes,' said Maya. I repeated, 'Eric is my real son and I must hug him.'

Maya nodded her head approvingly and cradled the other (girl) baby doll. After a while, the doll in Maya's arms started crying. 'You must comfort her,' said Maya. I put baby Eric down nicely, picked up Maya's crying baby doll and started to comfort her. The girl doll did not stop crying. I carried on comforting her and said that I loved her very much. After a few minutes, I asked why the baby doll was still so sad. Maya said that the doll feels very, very alone. 'Why is that?' I asked. Maya sniffed, 'I am totally alone and Eric isn't!'

I was shocked by Maya's intense reaction, but I tried to stay as calm as possible and to concentrate on the play. 'But I am holding you very tightly, baby, and I love you so much!' I said. 'Yes, but you are not her real mother, but you are Eric's real mother!'

Through Maya's play, it became clear to me that my daughter had the wrong notion about adoption. I was very glad to know this. Later on, when we talked about it, Maya told me that her friends repeatedly say that I am not her real mother. It also became evident that she is jealous of Eric.

In Chapter 7, I discuss how you might respond to your child if he thinks that you are not his real mother/father. I also discuss the confusing thoughts that adopted children may have about a sister or brother born to adopters.

When you engage in pretend play, always be sure that your child invents the story. He has to make the rules and you should stick to them. Always ask what your child wants you to say, and play enthusiastically. Try not to judge your child's play. You only need to guide him. Just name/identify the story or the creation he made; usually that is sufficient. You could ask a specific question, for example: 'Why is the mother doll so upset now?' or 'You have built a very tall castle. Can you tell me why it is so tall?'

By making space and time for your child's play, by watching it closely and by participating in it, you may learn how your child's understanding is developing, what dreams and fantasies he has, and how his feelings are changing or have changed.

Communicating through music, dance or movement

Children can also communicate their feelings through music, dance or movement. Does your child love music? What kind of music does he like the most? Does he like cheerful or melancholic music? Does he like a fast or a slow rhythm? You could ask him about the colour or the mood of his favourite music, for example, 'I feel sad when I listen to that song, do you?' In this way, a child becomes more aware of his feelings (examples quoted and re-translated from Dutch edition, Verrier, 2003, p. 151).

Maybe you can enter your child's inner world through dance or movement. The way in which children (and adults) move always says something about how they are feeling. Does your child move in an open, spontaneous way or does he move in an inhibited, careful way? Your child might move stiffly if he has a headache, a back or neck pain. Muscle strain is often a symptom of built-up emotional stress. If your child learns to be aware of his body, he can learn to find balance and to feel more safe. He may then dare to be more open about his feelings and thoughts.

A sport that focuses on body posture and control, like gymnastics, swimming, dance or a martial art, may help your child to better understand his feelings. He can learn that if he walks upright and confidently, he will also feel emotionally strong, or that he can make his body feel as light as a feather or as heavy as a mountain.

Responding to questions

The importance of being prepared

Adopted children become more aware of their background as they grow up; from nursery school on they will begin to ask questions. If you want to give them straight, well-considered answers, you must prepare yourself for possible questions.

In this chapter you will find many questions that adopted children ask their parents. The possible answers I suggest may initiate a way of thinking that will enable you to fit your answers to your child's history, temperament and family situation.

The age categories I use give only an indication about when your child may ask a question for the first time. She may ask these questions at a younger or older age, and they will most probably be repeated. The information suitable to tell your child will depend on her level of understanding and emotional development, therefore this chapter is linked with the contents of Chapter 2.

It is, of course, possible that your child will only rarely ask about her adoption. In this case, you should try to find out whether this is a result of a "healthy disinterest" that relates to her development and her temperament. The fact that your child very seldom asks questions about adoption doesn't always mean that she is not thinking about it. The level of a child's curiosity is often linked to the level of openness in the family: the more accessible and "normal" the adoption story is to your child, the greater the chance that she will ask questions about it.

General discussion pointers

Below is some general advice about how to approach and respond to your child's questions.

- Don't be scared of your child's questions. If you don't have an answer ready, you could always say that you totally understand why she has asked the question and that if you were in her situation you would also want to know. You could then say that you don't have an answer, but that you will give her one in an hour, tomorrow, in a while, next week or when she is old enough to understand, depending on the question and the situation.
- If your child asks a question, try to find out first exactly what she means. She may mean something different to what you think, or she may be looking for a much simpler answer than you imagine. A mother told me this story about her six-year-old son:

> My son and I were in a very busy supermarket. I was weighing some fruit when suddenly Aaron said: 'Mum, you bought me, didn't you?' I was shocked and told my son that we would talk about it when we got home. On the way home, I was wondering where Aaron got that idea from – maybe children at school had made nasty comments.
>
> When we arrived home, I asked Aaron about it and it appeared that they had read a book in school in which a little boy called Remi was sold by his father. Aaron

had compared this very different story to his own situation. I then explained to him that adoption is not the same as what happened to Remi in that story.

- If you want to find out what your child means, it is best to use affirmative, neutral sentences (see Chapter 5) that could be alternated with a direct question. Below is an example of a dialogue with a six-year-old child:

> *I don't want to have brown eyes.*
> *You would prefer your eyes to be another colour.*

> *Yes, I don't think my brown eyes are pretty.*
> *Why don't you think they are pretty?*

> *I want to have the same colour eyes as Jake.*

Here is another example of a discussion with a four-year-old child:

> *I wish I wasn't born out of the tummy of an India-mother.*
> *You don't like it that you came out of the tummy of an India-mother.*

> *No, I don't like that.*
> *You don't like that.*

> *No. I wish I was born out of your tummy.*
> *I understand that. I would have wanted that too. But a sweet India-mother carried you in her tummy. Would you like to be in my tummy now?*

> *Yes.*
> *Then come and sit under my jumper.*

- If your child asks a difficult question, that is a good sign. She obviously feels safe with you and doesn't think that the question is "too odd to ask".

- If you almost never talk about the adoption, the birth country or the birth parents, your child will probably find it more difficult to ask questions about it.

Frequently asked questions

From about 2½ or 3 years old

Where do children come from?

This is the most basic question. Many toddlers and young children will start asking this if they see their mother or somebody else pregnant. This provides adoptive parents with a good opportunity to start talking about adoption. If children don't ask the question themselves, you can easily start talking about it after seeing a pregnant woman, or by refering to a previous pregnancy of a relative or friend or your own (it may even be possible to show photos of this pregnancy or birth).

From about the age of two-and-a-half, children can understand quite well that babies come from a mother's tummy. You could play a game of putting one of your child's favourite dolls under your jumper and then letting the baby be born. The newborn baby cries, gets milk from the breast or from a bottle and is dressed in warm clothes. You can then expand on the story and tell your child that all babies are born out of their mother's tummy, and that your child came out of a Russian mother's tummy, for example. If you have a family with both birth and adopted children, you could explain that her sister came out of your own tummy. Young children will absorb these details without feeling fearful or unhappy. One adoptive mother described how she spoke to her daughter about her Korean mother:

> Kim (3) has an older brother, Dong (6), with whom we
> talk regularly about his adoption. She also has an older
> sister, Eva (8), who is our birth child. Kim loves to look

at photos of my big tummy from when I was pregnant with Eva. Suddenly, just before bedtime one day, she said: 'Kim Ko-ea-tummy-Mum-on.' I didn't understand her words. I thought that it had something to do with what had happened this morning when she was lying on my tummy in the bed, so I responded by saying: 'You lay on my tummy this morning.' But Kim repeated: 'Kim Ko-ea tummy.' It started to make a little sense to me and I said: 'You came out of a Korean mother's tummy.' Kim nodded, satisfied: 'Kim Ko-ea tummy-mother. Dong too.' I confirmed her words: 'You came out of a Korean-mother's tummy and Dong did too.' She carried on with 'Eva didn't, Eva Mummy's tummy.' I repeated again what she said: 'Yes, sweetheart. Eva came out of Mummy's tummy.' To this she replied 'Not nice!' And I said: 'You don't like it that Eva came out of Mummy's tummy and you didn't.' She agreed with that. 'You would have liked to have come out of Mummy's tummy too.' She nodded again and repeated several times that she and Dong came out of a Korean mother's tummy. And then she said: 'Mummy Daddy Kim Ko-ea fetch.' I smiled. Such a little girl, who already knows about where she came from. I was quite bewildered. She talked about it twice again, at bedtime. After that, the discussion was over.

Another adoptive mother described a dialogue she had with her daughters of five and three years old about "how babies grow in the tummy":

Han Yu (5) and Lin (3) were bathing together. Han Yu was studying her sister's navel in great detail. Han Yu had been fascinated by the human body for quite some time and already knew that babies grow in their mother's tummy. She wanted to know more about it and so we spoke about how a mother feeds the baby in her tummy through the umbilical cord. The fact that sandwiches were not eaten in the tummy was clear to her. 'The baby doesn't have a nappy on; it gets very dirty in your tummy, hey Mum?' We started talking about how she grew in her China mother's tummy. I then said that Han Yu and Lin also got food in the tummy and that their navels are the last piece of the umbilical cord. That made it all of a sudden very concrete for Han Yu; I saw it in her eyes. I said, 'But we don't know who that China-mother, was do we?' Until then, Han Yu had always responded by saying, 'It doesn't matter.' But this time, she became quiet for a moment. A little later they were having fun again in the bath. However, every now and then we take another little step towards the full realisation of what their adoption really means.

A question that may stem from this is:

Why did I grow in a Russia-mother's tummy and not in yours?

It will be enough if you say:

Your Russian mother could not care for you (even though she probably really wanted to).

Where do I come from?

This question doesn't have much meaning for toddlers. They do not yet have a developed sense of space. An answer like 'You come from a country far away' is still too abstract for them. "Birmingham" is just as far away as "the country over the ocean". However, it is good to regularly mention the name of the birth country. It can be useful to display a world map or a map of the birth country even though your child does not yet understand the concept of the "world". When your child reaches nursery school age, questions may follow:

Why do I come from Colombia?

Why don't I live in China?

Why didn't you leave me in Guatemala?

You can give a very basic answer to these questions by saying, for example:

Because your birth mother and father could not look after you.

Because they didn't have enough food.

After you have given a basic answer, distract your child if she is still too young to understand other information.

Can I get into your tummy?

If your child asks this, she probably indicates that she wants to be closer to you, and that is a good sign. She may want to initiate pretend-birth games. You can easily enter this game, and you can broaden it by pretending to breastfeed or by giving her a bottle and wrapping her up in a warm blanket.

Questions that may follow include: 'Was I in your tummy?', 'I came out of your tummy?' It is important that you always tell the truth, so that you don't have to go back on your words. If your child wants to pretend she was in your tummy, she can get under your jumper, and play-act being born. Although she really knows that she was in another woman's tummy, this can make her feel safe. Your child may say: 'I do not want to come out of another woman's tummy.' You can agree that it would have been nice if she had come out of your tummy, but it didn't happen that way. Now you can give her the opportunity to be in your tummy by playing the birth game. You could include the absent birth mother in the pretend game by saying that she probably loved the baby that grew in her tummy.

When she comes out from under your jumper, you can hug her and kiss her and say that both you and the birth mother are very happy that this baby is born. If you enter your child's fantasy play, very little can go wrong. When she is ready to stop the game, it is normally a sign that her need to think about her birth or to act it out has been fulfilled. As a result, her need to "be in your tummy" may be played and (re)discovered very often, without there being a distinction (in the play) between the one or the other child. During this play you can make clear to your adopted child that she is in your tummy now, but that in reality she was in her birth mother's tummy. Toddlers can register these different realities. If you accept both realities and talk frankly about both births, your child won't discover anything strange. Just like she doesn't find it strange that one child is a boy and the other child is a girl.

Was my brother/sister in your tummy?

This question is a result of everything your child has already heard about the birth and adoption. If her sister or brother is also adopted, you could again talk about the important role of the birth mother. It can be supportive to children if they know that their sister or brother also came out of another mother's tummy.

If your family has both adopted and birth children, you can explain the different ways in which children can come into a family.

Why did my older/younger sister/brother come out of your tummy?

You don't need to give toddlers a detailed answer. It is often the "why" itself that they pursue relentlessly at this age. You could just say:

> Mum and Dad wanted a child very much. That child grew in Mum's tummy and then Felix was born.

Try not to give a complicated answer if your child is not yet able to reason or you may be faced with an endless number of whys. Explain once again that she came out of her birth mother's tummy and that this mother could not take good care of her baby.

From about 4 or 5 years old

At this stage, it is important to encourage your child to ask questions and to answer simply and honestly. If you listen to your child and watch her while she is playing with dolls, talking to friends, drawing and so on, you may discover what she understands about her adoption.

Why couldn't my mother take care of me any more?

You can answer this question very simply. Work out one or two basic reasons beforehand, for example:

> *Because all parents in China are only allowed to have one or two children.*

> *Because in China parents get punished/fined if they have more than one or two children.*

> *Because your mother was far too young to care for a child.*

> *Because your mother was sick (or had no money, or was alone) (see Chapter 3).*

If you tell your child that her birth parents could not take care of her, it is important to talk about their feelings – this gives the birth parents a human dimension and shows your child that she is of value, not a thrown-away child. She will feel valued if she knows that her birth parents' decision to give her up for adoption was probably difficult and painful. You could say:

Your birth parents probably felt very sad when they gave you up for adoption.

It was probably very painful for them to have to give you up for adoption.

Questions like:

Why did you adopt me?

Why was I given up for adoption?

can be variations on this theme, although the first question is ambiguous, because it can also mean what was your motivation for adoption.

Why did you adopt me?

If your child wants to know why you wanted to adopt, you should be honest about it and talk at your child's cognitive and emotional level. This could start to build a strong basis of trust. Parents do not build trust only by being open and honest about their child's adoption history, but also by showing their own grief about their infertility, if this has been an important issue for them. It may sound contradictory, but your own sorrow may comfort your child; it could help her put her own sadness into perspective. Your child may learn that sometimes a door closes in life, but that as a result, another door opens that you would not want to have missed for anything in the world.

Why did you take me away?

Your child may simply mean 'Why did you adopt me?' She may, however, also be preoccupied with the terms "taking away", "buying" and "stealing". Maybe your child misinterprets the concept of adoption and it is therefore important to find out why she is asking this question.

First, convince your child that nobody just took her away. Then explain that her birth mother could not look after her and that she then gave her up for adoption. Highlight the point that she would have been adopted anyway, even if it wasn't by you.

Your child may then ask:

Can my mother come and fetch me again?

Even if your child never asks this question, it is important to regularly reassure her that you have signed official papers and will always be her parents. Nobody can take her away now or in the future.

How did I get to be with you?

Your child may have asked this question already, when she was younger. You most probably told her a beautiful, celebratory story about the day she joined your family. As your child gets older, you can expand on this story by explaining some of the more difficult aspects. You can add the detail, step-by-step.

Aren't you my real mother?

This question often follows comments other children have made. It is important to be aware that other children, even good friends, can make careless remarks. Even if your child doesn't ask, it is important to confirm that you are her real mother and father. Explain why some children in her class think that you are not her real parents:

> *Some children think that a mother is only a real mother if the child grew in the mother's tummy. They think that only your Russia-mother is your "real" mother. But that isn't so, because I am also your real mother and that's because you have been adopted. You grew in your real Russia-mother's tummy, but then you came to live with*

> us and now we take care of you and therefore we are
> also your real dad and mum.

Explain what "being adopted" means.

> If a child is adopted, like you are, they mostly have two
> fathers and two mothers: the parents you were born to
> and the parents who take care of you. Because the
> parents to whom you were born could not look after
> you, they searched for new parents who could take
> good care of you.

One adoptive mother used the following explanation for her six-
year-old daughter:

> If a new child comes into a family, this child's name
> must be written down in a big book called a register. All
> new children's names are written down in a register:
> children who were born in this city or town, as well as
> children who were born in countries far away and who
> then came to live with their new mum and dad. When
> you came into our family, your name was also written in
> that book. The fact that your name is in there proves
> that you are our real child and that we are your real
> mum and dad. You will always stay with us and nobody
> can take you away.

You could also add that your child also has another father and
mother, and that they are the birth parents. Another adoptive
mother offered the following explanation:

> Our children sometimes get teased at school; other
> children say to them that we are their "pretend
> parents". That isn't very nice, of course, but we are
> pleased to know what is being said because we are now
> able to talk about it. If somebody says to them that we
> are not their real parents, we have prepared our

children to ask: 'What does a real father and mother do for you then?' The children at school give an answer like: 'They make sure that I am not hungry, bring me to school, put me to bed and keep me safe, they give me presents, they comfort me when I am sad or sick.' Then my children say: 'My parents also do that for me, so they are my real parents. Only, I did not come out of my mother's tummy.' This mostly suffices.

I wish that I still lived in the country where I was born.

Children who are adopted at an older age sometimes long for their birth country where they had friends, where they knew the customs and the language and where they were used to different kinds of food, i.e. where they felt they belonged. Other older adopted children will do the opposite: they embrace their new family situation and do not want to go back to their birth country, even for a visit. Sometimes they are afraid that if they do go back, they will have to stay.

These feelings of loss or fear are often a sign that your child has started grieving about her adoption; at about age six or seven, adopted children begin to realise that they are different and that they were once abandoned. Some will first deny their emotions, others will become silent, angry or sad. During the coming weeks, months or years, different feelings of adoption-related grief may be expressed (see Chapters 8 and 9).

It is important not to deny what your child is feeling. It will not help to say that here you can get a proper education and there you can't; or here you have a family, while there you would have grown up in an orphanage without parents. Your child can't benefit from these arguments if she is in the middle of a grieving process. It might comfort you to know that although these grieving stages occur periodically, they are mostly temporary. If you are able to go along with your child's grieving process, there is a good chance that she can put her experience of loss into perspective.

Below are some more thoughts, comments and questions that may crop up during a period of grieving:

> *I don't want to be adopted.*

> *I wanted to come out of your tummy.*

> *I don't want to have brown skin.*

> *I don't ever want to go back.*

> *If we go to my birth country, will you bring me back home with you?*

> *I want to go back to my real parents, they are probably nicer.*

> *How are my birth parents doing?*

> *Why did my older or younger sister/brother come out of your tummy?*

Your child may want to know why you have a family with both adopted and birth children. At first you can explain just like you would to a toddler:

> *Because we wanted to have a child. That child grew in my tummy and then Felix was born.*

You can then go on to explain your reasons for adoption in an honest, simple way:

> *We wanted to have another child very much, but Mum got sick after Felix was born, and then another child*

could not grow in her tummy. So we chose to adopt a child, and that child was you.

We wanted another child very much, but we didn't think it was necessary to have a second baby that would grow in Mum's tummy. We preferred to adopt a child.

We thought that we couldn't have children of our own, and so we decided to adopt a child. After we adopted you, a baby grew in Mum's tummy. That baby became Felix (also see Chapter 3).

From about 7 or 8 years old

Why was I given up for adoption?

This will be the key question at this stage. Children become interested in the world around them at this age, and they also become more aware that they were relinquished by their birth parents. Most adopted children will start grieving about their adoption at this age (see Chapters 8 and 9). You may be surprised by your child's sadness or anger because until now she had almost always seemed happy with the fact that she was adopted.

At this age, you can go into this question with a little more detail. Children are now able to understand that their birth parents did not have money, that they did not have enough food, that they were too young or alone and unmarried, that they were sick, or that they had died. However, it is important to emphasise that this does not mean that all parents who don't have money or who become sick will have to give their children up for adoption.

Your child may use words that sound harsh. You could hear her say to a friend, 'I was sent away by my birth mother', or 'I was given away when I was very young'. Ask her at an appropriate moment what she means when she uses the words "sent away". It may be just her way of saying "given up for adoption", but perhaps she

means something else: "being sent away" could carry the idea of
punishment. It is important that your child understands that the
adoption was not meant as punishment. Try to talk about her birth
parents regularly and assure your child that she was not naughty
and that her parents did not want to punish her by giving her up for
adoption.

Did my mother (father) love me?

Questions about the birth parents (at this stage mostly about the
birth mother) flow logically from your child's growing awareness
that she was once given up for adoption.There is a strong possibility
that she will convince herself that she caused the adoption: adopted
children often think that they weren't nice, healthy or beautiful
enough, or that they were the wrong sex. You can explain to your
child that it was not she as a person who was given up for
adoption, but that a baby was given up for adoption; in many cases,
birth parents decide to put their baby up for adoption even before it
is born. Questions in the same category are:

>   *Wasn't I nice enough to keep?*

>   *If I wasn't so nice or beautiful when I was a baby, would
>   you still have adopted me?*

>   *Did my parents not like me?*

>   *Was I ugly and sick and was that the reason why I was
>   given up for adoption?*

Certainly not all children will ask these questions. However, this
doesn't mean that they are not thinking about these issues.
Therefore, at this age it is important that you regularly confirm to
your child that under no circumstances was she responsible for her
adoption.

Watkins and Fisher emphasise that adopted children also want to hear that their birth parents wanted and loved them, and that they were not rejected by them (1993, p. 80). It is therefore best to tell your child that her birth parents most probably think about her often. In fact, this need to be wanted by both sets of parents is in a certain way comparable to the needs of children of divorced parents: they also benefit most if they are frequently told and shown that they are loved and wanted by both Mum and Dad, and that they will never have to choose between them. Be aware of the birth parent's situation: for social, cultural or personal reasons they may not want to have anything to do with their child. In order to avoid disappointment at a later stage, you could say:

I can't imagine that your parents don't think of you.

If your child talks negatively about her birth parents, it is important that you remain neutral. It is best to objectively name/identify your child's feelings or acknowledge it (confirmation of receipt) (Step 1, see Chapter 5). Preferably don't give your own opinion on what she has said. In this way your child will keep the freedom to change her mind about her parent(s) the next day, if she wants, and to share this with you. If you remain neutral in terms of your child's feelings, she may not experience loyalty conflicts and as a result she will probably feel safe to talk about her feelings.

What does my birth mother (father) look like?

As adopted children grow older and become more aware of the existence of their genetically related family, they will be curious about what their birth parents look like. Some children have a picture of their birth parents; others may have only a fantasy image.

If children have photographs, they won't have extremely deviating fantasies about what their birth parents look like; however, they may have deviating fantasies about their character, their talents, their motives for abandoning them, etc. These children could, for example, benefit from regularly drawing fantasy images of their birth parents in their own environment. If they do this, you may be able to start an open dialogue with your child about her fantasies about her birth parents and the circumstances in which they live.

If your child does not have photographs of her birth parents or if she hasn't yet made any fantasy drawings about them, you could stimulate your child to start doing this at this age, even if she does not express an explicit interest in it. The longer you wait, the stronger your child's fantasies may become. As a result, her fantasies may get more and more intense and then it becomes more and more difficult to start a dialogue about them.

If your child only experiences positive fantasies, you may want to keep it that way, even if the circumstances surrounding her birth parents are not so positive. At appropriate moments, you could highlight the less positive aspects, so that your child does not lose sight of reality. However, always try to ensure that your child does not get a negative feeling about what you tell her. She probably needs these positive fantasies because she is already very much aware of the less positive aspects.

Your child's fantasies about the birth parents can also be negative, for example, if your child has unpleasant memories of the period before the adoption took place. She may have only negative feelings about her birth parents (she may even want to deny their existence completely). In this case, it is even more important that she talks with you about her fantasies. If she is able to talk about her unpleasant memories in a safe environment, there may even be opportunities to talk about some of the positive memories.

If your child has extreme positive or negative fantasies, it may be best to call in the help of an expert who has experience in adoption-related issues.

Is she my real mother (father) (and you aren't)?
Your child probably has already asked this question at a younger age. Continue to reassure her that you are her real and forever

parents. On the one hand, it is important that your child learns to understand that you and her birth parents signed legally valid, official papers and that no one can simply come and fetch her. On the other hand, it is also important that she learns that, in fact, she does have two sets of parents, namely the birth parents and the parents who care for her now and who will remain her parents throughout her life. By talking about the birth parents on an equal basis, you give your child the confidence that she needs to be able to talk and fantasise about them. Even if she knows that she may never meet them, she owes her existence to them and because she is one hundred per cent genetically related, she will be connected to them for her whole life (see also earlier section, 'Aren't you my real mother?').

Why didn't you give my parents money?

Some children may ask this question from about age eight or nine; others may come up with it earlier. Try always to give a clear answer.

Most children are given up for adoption not only out of poverty, but also as a result of cultural or social taboos. In other situations the mother could not keep her child because there was no father, or the parents were too young or mentally or physically ill. Explain to your child that her birth parents gave her up for adoption not only because they had no money, but also because they didn't know how to look after a child. Also explain that money alone is not enough to be able to raise a child. Ask a question (depending on your child's level of understanding): 'If a rich mother is sick and alone, do you think she will be able to look well after her child?' Your child will most probably answer: 'Yes, if she gets some help.' You could then ask if the mother would also be able to do this without any help.

You may also use this question to discuss the topic of what raising a child actually means. For example, you could ask her what she understands about raising a child and what she thinks parents need to do to make sure that their child grows up properly. Through conversation, it becomes clear that money is not enough to be able to raise a child.

Did you buy me?

At some point, children adopted from overseas will understand that their adoption has cost you a lot of money. This may be when you are in the process of adopting again, or it may come up during an adoption conversation with your child.

Be sure to tell your child yourself that her adoption cost a lot of money. If she hears it from someone else or if you wait until she is older, she may be shocked by this fact. Explain that all overseas adoptions cost a lot of money because children have to be placed into new families very carefully. Everyone has to be sure that the birth parents really want their child to be adopted. Tell her that one part of the money has to be paid to adoption agencies and lawyers. The adoption agencies use the money to employ people who are able to guide the adoption process properly. The lawyers use the money to ensure that everything is correctly done – they make sure that all the documentation is official and signed by all the people who are involved.

You could go on to explain that some of the money was paid to the orphanage or the foster family with whom your child lived, so that other children would have food and a safe place to stay.

Finally, you could say that the journey to the birth country also cost you money: you had to book the flights, buy food and pay for the hotel; if you didn't bring your child home yourself, and instead she was escorted, you had to pay the best people you could find to bring your child to her new homeland.

I wish that I had stayed in my birth country.

At this age it is important that you support your child in the sadness that she is possibly experiencing as a result of the adoption. Validate your child's feelings and regularly confirm to her that you have noticed her sadness. Give her permission to discuss how she feels. The feeling of loss may last for only a short period, but it can also last longer. Much depends on your child's temperament, and how you handle her sadness (see Chapters 8 and 9). If your child seems to be homesick, suggest that you could go to her birth country for a holiday. Such a trip may be less difficult for her before the onset of puberty, as she is still strongly centered on the family. Decide together whether to visit the birth country or not.

According to Holly van Gulden and Lisa Bartels-Rabb, it is more complicated to travel to the native country during puberty, as teens are separating and pulling away from the family on their way toward adulthood. As teens pull away, they need a strong sense that their parents still want them. If left until adolescence, visits and searches can stress this separation process. Your teen may think that you want to go back to her previous home because you would like her to go back where she came from. According to van Gulden and Bartels-Rabb, younger children are better able to take in the experience and information offered without misconstruing the message, but they still need to be told that you are just going there on a holiday or that your search is to gather information and not to return them to their birth parents (2001, pp. 202–203).

I wanted to be adopted by other parents.

At this age, many children, adopted or not, fantasise about other, more ideal parents (see also Chapter 2) – imaginary parents who very seldom say no to their children, and who never punish them or make them do homework. These fantasies normally fade as children learn that nobody is perfect, neither they themselves, nor their parents.

For adopted children, however, these fantasies are more complicated, as they become aware that they might have ended up living in another family, in another country with a completely different family lifestyle. Your child may wonder what it would have been like being part of another family. These fantasies are probably temporary and can be compared to the fantasies that other children have about more ideal parents.

Ensure that you don't only tell your child that it was "meant to be", or that you were "destined to be together" – this might seem like a comfort in the short term, but there are some pitfalls to this (see 'A few notes on destiny', p. 172). It is better to say: 'It was probably meant to be that you came into this family, but I can't know for sure.'

Validate your child's fantasies that she could also have been adopted by another family. These thoughts are just as real as the thought that she might have been left behind at the orphanage. Also remind her that the situation cannot be changed and that you are her forever parents. You can validate her feelings by saying, for example, that you can imagine that she doesn't like it, rather than saying that you agree with her feelings. You could ask her what the other parents would add to her life. Try to find out what she would like about other adoptive families. The fact that they live far away in a warm climate? Or that they have many sisters and brothers, or a big house? Encourage your child to express her fantasies and wishes by talking, drawing or playing. If you name/identify her fantasies without judging them, she will most probably integrate these feelings in her identity and outgrow them.

My real mother is probably a lot nicer.
Your child may fantasise about other, more ideal adoptive parents, and also, of course, about her birth parents. These more or less unknown parents will seem preferable, simply because they are not the ones who are bringing her up.

Validate your child's fantasies and talk about them with her regularly in a sensitive and responsive way. Your child may need these positive fantasies in order to put her adoption into perspective. She may move from fantasy to the feeling that 'Because my birth mother is nice, she must have loved me very much.' This is a healthy thought that can help your child to accept her adoption and to love two sets of parents. Your child might also use her fantasy to stop feeling pain and anger about her relinquishment. A positive fantasy can be a defense mechanism: your child will only allow herself to feel the anger and sadness once she is ready to do so (see Chapters 8 and 9).

If your child holds on to her fantasies for a very long time, it might be a good idea to mention the reality now and again. You may know some facts about the birth parents that are less positive; you don't need to emphasise them, but you could talk about them (at her level) in a neutral way. Your child might feel the need to deny it for a while, but the moment will come when she has to face reality to come to terms with her past. You could say, for example:

> Your birth mother is probably very nice. I think that she is good at sport, just like you. Maybe we will look for her when you are older. But you should also know that she is sick/that she didn't look after her children properly/that she put you in danger/that she might have a family of her own and that you might never meet her.

Some children have totally negative fantasies about their birth parents. They too are denying the reality. It is equally important to validate these negative feelings. Denying reality, either negatively or positively, often serves an important function in the process of coming to terms with the past. As your child grows older, she will learn to understand that no one is only good or bad (and neither is she).

You may feel that your child's positive fantasies are a rejection of you as her parent. However, her behaviour is easy to interpret. By having these positive fantasies she is not saying that she doesn't trust you or love you, but that she feels loyal to her (unknown) birth parents. Try to discover what kinds of fantasies your child has about her birth parents and try to talk about them together.

Who was my father? Where is my father/mother now? How are my parents doing?

From about the age of seven or eight, many adopted children will want to know more about their birth parents. How are they doing? Are they happy? A real interest in the birth father develops at about age nine or ten, although some children do ask questions about him at a younger age. What kind of person was he and was he involved in the adoption process? If you only know a little about the birth father, be careful not to stereotype him. If the birth father was not married to the birth mother, it does not mean that he left her or never thought about the mother and child again: he may have felt guilty, unhappy or frustrated. He may have assumed that after he left he had no rights any longer as a father or any say about the future of his child.

Other family-type questions that your child might be preoccupied with from about the age of eight are:

> *What kind of work do my birth parents do?*

> *What do they look like?*

> *Do they look like me?*

> *Do they think about me?*

> *Do you think my parents are happy?*

> *Why couldn't my father stay with my mother?*

> *Do I have more family (sisters, brothers, grandparents)?*

> *What do my sisters and brothers look like?*

If you have spoken openly together about the birth parents from the start, these questions will be a logical continuation of the adoption dialogue. The answers you have given before probably do not suffice any longer for your child, or it may be that she feels that there are no more questions to be asked; that most topics have been dealt with already.

It is, however, important to try to get into the "new" inner world of your child, because by this age she has developed much more awareness of her adoption. You could speculate together about her possibly inherited talents and resemblances and about how her birth parents might be living. Tell your child that her birth parents probably think about her and that they almost certainly would want to know how she is doing. Even if her birth parents were not sick or had mistreated her, let her know that, nevertheless, they probably also miss her. If your child can believe that, despite painful facts and being relinquished, she was also loved and wanted by her birth parents, she is more likely to develop a healthy, positive self-image and to allow herself to be angry or sad about her past. Be careful not to say 'Your mother gave you up for adoption because she loved you so much' (see Chapter 2).

Why can't they be in contact with me?

Many children who have the name and/or photo of (one of) their birth parents, will ask this question. Try to provide a simple answer, for example:

> When your parents gave you up for adoption, they signed papers that said they were not allowed to contact you. Birth parents can't just phone or write letters to their children (this is the case with closed adoptions; contacts are mostly arranged by the adoption agencies). Most adoptions have been organised in this way because adopted children are then able to grow up in a safe environment without being asked difficult questions by their birth parents; children mostly can't reply with the right answers. When you are older, you can decide for yourself whether you would like to write to or to meet your birth parents.

Your child may periodically want to make a note of questions she would like to ask her birth father or mother. You could store these questions with other items like letters and drawings your child has made.

You love my brother/sister more because he/she is actually your own child.

These comments are made in almost every family that has adopted as well as birth children. Remember that almost all children, adopted or not, compare the amount of love and attention they get from their parents to see what differences or similarities there are. This begins even when children are toddlers.

By making this claim, your child is expecting you to rebut it. She wants validation that you love all the children in the family equally; she probably does not always feel sure about this. This may be as a result of her different skin colour or temperament, or because of her background; maybe she feels like a second choice in comparison to her brother or sister. In all such cases, your child is looking for your loyal confirmation that all the children in this family are equally wanted and loved. You may convince her if you get into her inner world:

> *Do you remember when Snowy was the only rabbit here? You thought no other rabbit could be as nice. Then we got Spotty. In the beginning, you still thought Snowy was nicer, but after a short time, you couldn't choose between them, because you liked them both. And then Snowy had babies, and then it was even more difficult to choose, do you remember? She had ten babies! And then you also loved all the little ones. That is how it was for us too. In the beginning only Dad was here and I loved him very much and he loved me too. I thought that I would never be able to love someone as much as I loved him. But then I got pregnant and your brother was born and then we both loved him very*

much. We realised that you can love one person very much, but at the same time you can love someone else as much. A few years later, when we adopted you, we loved you just as much as we loved your brother. It never mattered to us that you did not come out of my tummy. We love you both equally, even though you are both very different. Dad is also very different, but I love him very much too.

By telling this story you are also teaching your child that she can love her birth parents too.

If you have a birth child, don't suppress the story of the birth out of loyalty towards your adopted child(ren). Ensure that both stories are given equal importance. By doing so, your children can see that you do not make a distinction between the two.

You would rather have had a child of your own.
Some children confront their parents with this, others only think about it, and for some children the thought has simply not entered their minds.

If your child makes a comment like this, try to talk about it realistically and honestly. Your child probably needs reassurance from you. She wants to hear that you did want her, and that you love her one hundred per cent and that you would not want to lose her for anything in the world. To get this message across, it is usually not enough just to say it. Make it clear to her that you were sad about not being able to have a child in your tummy. Teach her that sometimes in life things don't work out the way people want them to, but that this doesn't mean they are not happy with the way they turn out in the end. Sometimes a child may not be able to attend a professional ballet class because she isn't strong enough, but afterwards she learns to play the clarinet and now she really enjoys it. Or sometimes a child loses her best friend because she moves to another town and she misses her very much, but after a while it seems that another girl in her class can also be a very good friend. This friendship may be different, but it doesn't have to be less close.

Always try to teach your child that, when it comes to feelings, it is not a question of "either/or", but rather of "this and that". You can be sad about something, but at the same time be happy about something else. In this way, your child might also learn that she may long for her birth parents, but this does not mean that she is rejecting you.

From about 9 or 10 years old

From about age 10 (pre-puberty), children become more perceptive. Your child will probably argue about everything and seriously begin to undermine your authority. It is important to hear not only her confrontational questions and comments about her adoption, but also about social and political injustice in general. Try to be prepared for her questions, so that you are able to discuss them with her seriously and be able to stay calm if it gets difficult.

By the time your child has finished junior school, you should have told her all she needs to know about her adoption. If there are painful facts you have not yet discussed, you should try to do it now. If you are not sure whether your child is able to cope with certain details, then you should ask an adoption expert for advice.

I won't listen to you because you are not my real mother.
Almost all adopted children over the age of eight will say to their parents at least once that they don't have the right to tell them what to do because they are not their real father and mother, or they will comment that they actually love their real mother more. Don't be shocked. All pre-teens, adopted or not, want to undermine their parents' authority. "Normal" children use other metaphors and tactics, but actually they are fighting the same battle, namely, growing up to be an adult. To grow up, they need to be able to

stand up for themselves and cope on their own. Therefore, they need to develop their own identity.

Pre-teens are often fascinated by differences and similarities between people and in searching for their own identity they will develop a bond with sometimes very different children/adults compared to their parents and siblings. This development may distress you, especially if your child asserts her autonomy with anger. As an adoptive parent, you may feel more vulnerable because there is no blood tie and you may fear that your child will abandon you one day.

Try to put these insecure feelings aside, stay calm and ascertain why your child seems to be against you. Maybe she is angry about something in particular or perhaps it is related to the general confusion that stems from the onset of puberty. Your child may also mean the exact opposite with her dismissive behaviour: she may actually want you to reassure her that she can stay with you forever, that you have a permanent bond, a bond that automatically exists between people in genetically related families. She can be just as scared about being abandoned by you because she isn't nice enough. In addition, she may also be looking for support and help because she is trying to love two sets of parents.

Try always to react in a sensitive and responsive way; it might become clear that there are other reasons for this behaviour. Always be aware that not all behaviour is caused by the fact that your child was adopted.

Why couldn't my parents take care of me?
From about age nine, children are generally quite able to understand why they were given up for adoption. It is important that you tell your child the truth even if the facts are painful, otherwise she might build up fantasies that are incorrect. The shock will be much greater if she hears the truth when she is older. However, always try to talk about the reasons at your child's level of

understanding. Instead of telling her that girls in her birth country are less valued than boys, tell her something about the country's culture and how this puts a burden on some families. The same may apply if your child was given up for adoption because she was illegitimate; children are often given up for adoption to avoid a scandal for the family, even if the mother wants to keep her child.

Show your child the official documents, tell her about the adoption procedure and other details. At this age, she is perfectly capable of understanding what an adoption agency is and why this agency got involved in the process. If your child gets the opportunity as a pre-teen to read and look at the official adoption documentation, she may absorb the details more naturally and be less shocked about the content than when she is older. If the reasons for adoption are very painful and you don't feel sure about telling your child, it may be best to consult an adoption specialist.

If your child expresses anger about the adoption, it is important to find out whether the anger is aimed at the birth parents themselves, or at the distressing circumstances in which they lived and in which they were compelled to relinquish their child. If your child is able to distinguish between these two feelings, it will help her to develop a positive attitude towards her birth parents and to accept that, unfortunately, they had no choice. One question that may arise from the abovementioned question is:

> *Why was I adopted and my sisters and brothers were not?*

How are they doing?
At this age, your child may become more interested in all the members of her birth family and it is important to encourage her to talk or ask about them. Always talk openly about brothers and sisters. If possible, try to give detailed information about why the birth parents had to give up their first, third or fifth child for

adoption. Tell your child that this does not mean that her birth parents loved her less. If you don't know whether there are more siblings, promise your child that you will try to find out later on.

How much did you have to pay for me? Why didn't you give that money to my parents instead of taking me away? Why don't you support them now?

Pre-teens can be critical and they expect honest answers to these kinds of questions. Explain how much money you had to pay and why an adoption is so expensive (see previous section, 'Did you buy me?'). Tell her that her birth parents had very little money but that this was only one of the reasons they had to give up their child for adoption. Another important reason was that at that moment in their lives they were not capable of taking care of a child properly (see 'Why didn't you give my parents money?'). Tell your child that she would have been given up for adoption regardless.

If you haven't yet offered any help to the orphanage or foster family, tell your child why you haven't done so. You may be supporting other projects in her birth country or elsewhere, or maybe it is not possible to provide support because of political or cultural circumstances. If it is allowed, it may be important to your child to make a concrete plan now for those who have stayed behind. Ask your child how she would like to support them and get her actively involved in this; for instance, she may want to collect money or clothing from children in her class or she may want to donate some of her pocket money. By participating in a support programme, you can show that your interest in the orphanage or the (foster) family did not end when you adopted your child. Be aware, however, that donations given directly to the orphanage and/or families can result in regular personal requests for financial support.

Why can only rich people adopt?

If adoption costs a lot of money, it means that only people who have enough can afford it. Agree in a pragmatic way. Yes, there are people who earn too little to be able to adopt a child from overseas. Agree with your child that this is unfair, but that on the other hand you can't do anything about it. It isn't the children you have to pay for, but the procedures and the travel arrangements, which are very expensive. It would be nice if adoption from overseas were free, but it isn't.

Are my parents OK...they aren't unhappy?

When you adopted your child, you probably received information about the birth family. This may include all or some family, medical and social details (nationalities, names, addresses, family situation, physical health, marital status, work, reason for the adoption, etc). Usually, there is no contact with the birth parents after the adoption, and therefore you are unlikely to know how they are. It is best just to tell your child what you do know; and then to suggest what may have happened after the adoption took place.

> *Your parents were not married to each other. Your father was a businessman and your mother was married to another man. They had children who are your half-sisters and brothers. When we went to adopt you, your parents were both doing well, but they were very sad that they had to give you up for adoption. I hope that your parents are still well and that they are both happy and healthy. I can't imagine that they don't think about you; they are probably very curious about how you are doing. In a few years, we could perhaps look for them, if you want to.*

If your child's parents were mentally or physically ill at the time of the adoption, or very poor and/or addicted to drugs or alcohol, you could try to include some hope in what you say:

> *They may be doing a little better now than they were*
> *then. I hope so, in any case. If you want to, we could*
> *look for your birth parents when you are older, if you*
> *want to.*

Tell your child that she does not have to look for her birth parents if she doesn't want to. She may still be very angry with her father or mother for abandoning her. It is important that you always validate her angry or sad feelings. Don't make your child feel guilty about her parents by telling her too often that the birth parents were sick or poor and that they were probably very sad because they had to abandon their child. Try to say something like this:

> *I'm sure that your birth parents miss you, but I'm also*
> *sure that they are comforted by the fact that you are*
> *now with a forever family who takes good care of you.*

If you don't know the birth family because the child was a foundling, be honest and clear in your answer:

> *I don't know how your parents are doing. When we*
> *adopted you we didn't even know their names. I hope*
> *that they are doing well, but of course I don't know*
> *that for sure. We may be able to find out more in the*
> *future, but most probably we will never know.*

Search for books, films or documentaries that show something of the way of life or the political and social context in which the people in your child's birth country live.

Why was I adopted and all the other children in the orphanage were not? That isn't fair.

Your child may experience "survival guilt" because she was adopted by chance, while other children, as a result of that same fate, had to stay behind. Whatever answer you give, it is likely that none of them will put her mind at ease. Fate is always unpredictable –

sometimes it's wonderful and sometimes unkind. It is just like that, and nobody knows why. One person has good luck and the other does not. You may find a solution by telling your child 'You were destined to live with us', or 'It was meant to be.' But always be cautious with this type of reasoning (see 'A few notes on destiny', p. 172). Your child also needs to learn to accept her fate, however young she is. You could say:

> *I think that you were lucky compared to the children who stayed behind at the orphanage. But on the other hand, you haven't always had good luck, because you were put in the orphanage in the first place. You may feel powerless about helping these children; I would understand that. It is sad for the children who had to stay behind. But perhaps they aren't unhappy, because they can play and grow up together.*

Some children really worry about this and can, for example, develop eating disorders because of it, while others become depressed or destructive. If you notice this kind of behaviour, ask an adoption expert for advice. If your child feels sad every now and again but is happy and cheerful at other times, then she is probably concerned in a "healthy" way. Try to find out whether she would like to support the children who had to stay behind and help her to make a plan. You could consider travelling to the country of her birth so that your child can visit the children who live in the orphanage now.

My sister is lucky because she knows who her real mother is. It is not fair that I don't know who my mother is.

All children, whether adopted or not, compare their position in the family and their qualities and achievements with those of their siblings. Not everything is fairly shared out in the world, and one child may be able to accept these differences more easily than another. However, your child must learn to deal with the unfair differences.

Be honest and clear about your children's different stories. Let them know that it doesn't matter to you why a child was given up for adoption, or whether you know who the parents are or not. Tell them that you love them equally for who they are. Tell the child who made this comment that nothing can be changed about her story and assure her that in a few years you will try together to gather as much information as possible. But don't give your child false hope, and always be clear about what might be possible or not. If her sister/brother's story is more positive, don't cover it up. Let them know that different situations can exist side by side. Each child must learn to cope with her own strengths and weaknesses, with her own good or bad luck.

A few notes on destiny

From about the age of eight, children start to realise that only a very small part of the world is rich and that many children and parents live in less favourable circumstances. Adopted children may feel intensely that they could just as easily have grown up in the poor environment of their birth parents, or been adopted and moved to another part of the world, or stayed at the orphanage. As suggested above, you may tell your child that she and not another child was meant to be with you. You might say this because you want to put your child's mind at ease, or because you somehow believe in destiny. However, your child might interpret what you have said in a very different way to what you intended. She may think: 'What makes me so special that I am here and the other children are not?' This may even reinforce her idea that the world is not fair. Which god or system can give one child a good future while others must live in poverty without love?

The idea of destiny may also encourage your child to start thinking that because she is special she has to live up to special expectations. Children who have been adopted from orphanages were all "chosen" in some way; if not by the parents, then by the staff from the orphanage. Children could start asking themselves: 'Why did they choose me?', 'Was I always well behaved?', 'What would have happened if I hadn't smiled all the time…would they have chosen another child?' Your child might then feel that she always has to keep up the nice, cheerful front that predestined her to be chosen.

You may also unknowingly suggest that your child must be thankful to somebody or something for their destiny. As a result, she may not dare to feel angry or sad about being relinquished and put up for adoption. Thoughts about fate and fairness are linked to a specific period of development and are mostly temporary, but you must be careful if you want to reassure your child. It is better to say that maybe it was destined to be, but that you are not sure.

Dealing with questions at school

When adopted children attend primary school, they may get confronted with comments about their adoption. Sometimes these comments are amiable, but at other times they can be nasty or unpleasant. Perhaps a friend at school tells your child that adoption means that she was abandoned on the street by her parents. All adopted children are sometimes faced with embarrassing questions or remarks.

- Try to remain calm at these moments. Apart from the fact that children can often use brutal language, these comments are undoubtedly not meant the way you may think they are.
- Explain to your child that many people, both children and adults, do not understand precisely what adoption is and that they sometimes get things wrong. If your child really was found on the street, don't deny this, but add that her parents probably thought very carefully about where they would leave their baby because they wanted her to be in a safe place where someone would find her very quickly. Tell her that her birth parents didn't just leave her in the street, but that they wrapped her in a pretty blanket or put her in a basket by a tree or in a warm doorway. Let her know that in future she will be faced with more remarks about her adoption, but that

they are not meant to hurt her; they are often made out of ignorance. Reassure her that she can always talk to you about unkind comments because you can always explain to her exactly what happened.

- Your child might tell you that she was teased at school about her looks or her being adopted. Ask her precisely what was said in order to give her the chance to describe the incident in detail, and ask how she felt at that moment. Children are often better able to identify their feelings after the event. Ask her what happened next, what she did or said. Ask her whether she is happy with the way she handled the situation. In this way, your child can learn to review her own behaviour, so that she can react in the same or in a different way if it happens again.

- If your child is regularly being teased about her adoption, talk to her teacher. It may be a good time to discuss your child's adoption in class. Be aware that most young children will quickly forget what you have told them. It is therefore best to repeat the discussion when they are in a higher class and at a different level of understanding.

- Perhaps you could encourage the teacher to start a project that focuses on another country/the country your child came from, or on discrimination. Ask your child if she would like to start this and if so, which role she would like to play in presenting it.

- Ask the teacher if he or she would like to consider discussing family structures in class. Children can learn that there are different kinds of families and that one kind is no better than another. Children may live in one-parent families, foster or adoptive families, or with divorced, unmarried or same-sex parents. This should help your child to feel less different to others and help all the children to learn to be tolerant of others.

- Help to organise a celebration at school with cultural customs and food from your child's birth country. Perhaps the class could hear a recording of "Happy Birthday" in Spanish or Russian, or your child could talk about traditional flags or clothes from their country of origin. Perhaps dolls from a range of cultures could be used in a puppet play.

- If you notice discriminatory or racist behaviour in your child's school, discuss this with the head teacher immediately in order to stop it from happening.

Dealing with reactions of strangers

Adoptive families are regularly confronted with comments or questions, not only from their neighbours, family and friends, but also from total strangers. These questions are sometimes good natured and well intentioned, but they can also be rude or intrusive. Adoptive families may be faced with persistent prejudice from people who apparently think that they can ask this "minority ethnic family" whatever they feel like.

Below are some of the difficult questions/comments that people may ask:

Is he yours?

Oh, what a sweetie, where does she come from?

Did you adopt this child?

He should be grateful to you!

Are they real sisters?

Well, she doesn't need to sunbathe!

I just heard that orphans in China are all tied to their beds.

Is she one of those Chinese girls who was supposed to be aborted?

It is hard to imagine why someone would want to get rid of this child, isn't it?

She speaks her new language quite well, doesn't she?

How will he learn his new language skills?

She is still so young, she probably doesn't remember anything.

She has been here for a year now, so I presume she has forgotten all about Colombia.

Are you going to tell him that he was adopted?

She will want to go and look for her real parents later on. Won't that be hard for you?

What a sweet little girl. Pity she will have problems later.

It is good that you got him so young; you will probably have fewer problems later on.

Can you love her like your own?

Why was he given up for adoption?

Oh, poor thing! She only has one hand. Couldn't you have chosen another one?

What a beautiful child. Did you choose him yourself?

How much did you have to pay?

Couldn't you have children of your own?

It is nice that so many girls are coming out of Asia at the moment: they are still very young and the Chinese tend to adapt very quickly.

You don't know what you are bringing home.

Do you have a lot of information about him? Will you ever tell him everything?

Do you know the real parents? Have you met them?

Almost all adoptive families hear similar remarks and questions. It would be nice if it were possible to formulate standard answers, but each situation, each person and each adoption story is different. Here are a few guidelines that can help you to cope with difficult questions and comments.

- Be clear about your child's adoptive status. Remember that your child is your most important audience. If you answer questions clearly, and help her cope with them positively, your answers may guide her when she has to deal with questions on her own.
- Decide beforehand what you do and do not want to tell. Don't say anything because you want to be polite – your answers contain private information about your child. If an acquaintance or stranger asks: 'How much do you know about her real parents?' you could say: 'You mean her birth parents? We are very satisfied with what we know about them.'
- If someone asks whether your child is adopted and you don't want to talk about it, then reply in a calm, friendly way with another question: 'Why do you want to know?' If people say that they are merely curious, then just say 'Oh!' and start talking about something else. If people tell you they are thinking about or planning an adoption, you could discuss that with them.
- It is fine if you don't answer a question, or if you answer a question only partially. Start talking about something else if you don't want to give an answer. Smile and say: 'Shall we talk about something else?' or 'We prefer to talk about that at home.'
- If someone keeps pressing you for information about your child, you could then say: 'I value your interest, but I'm afraid that it is my child's private information.'
- You can use humour (if it suits you). If someone asks whether your

daughters are real sisters, you could answer that they are certainly not made of plastic. Test their "realness" (pre-discussed with your children) by lightly pinching their arm and then letting your children scream out aloud. A realistic answer like 'Now they are!' may also put an end to the conversation.

- Give answers that teach people something about adoption in general. If someone comments: 'I've heard that the back of Chinese children's heads are flat because as babies they have to lie on their backs', then you could say: 'We'd also heard about that, but it wasn't a problem at all. Children in Chinese orphanages are mostly cared for very well. The media only reports the negative facts and not what it's really like.'
- Learn from the time you were faced with a difficult question and didn't give the best possible answer. Don't be too hard on yourself. Don't blame yourself if you say the wrong thing – you will do better next time.
- Try to remember that most difficult questions are asked out of ignorance: the only thing that many people know, or think they know, about adoption is that adopted children will one day want to search for their "real" parents.
- See difficult questions as an opportunity to explain what adoption really is. If you talk positively about it, you may eliminate a few prejudices.
- Remember that you are not alone. All adoptive parents and all adult adoptees are confronted by intrusive questions, just as disabled people, older people and members of minority groups are. Compare your child's status with the one of a child with one hand. People tend to make the same difficult comments to these children: 'You can do a lot with that hand!' or 'Oh, shame!' and 'Can you eat with one hand or ride your bike?'
- If you are able to accept that you will be asked difficult questions, you will be able to cope with them a lot better.

Making your child resilient

Below are a number of tips that may help your child to respond adequately to difficult questions:

- Explain to your child that difficult questions are usually asked out of ignorance. Most people know very little about adoption; they often don't even realise what they are asking.
- Teach your child that she may tell adults that she doesn't want to talk about it. If she is afraid to do so in public, consider arranging a secret code: a sentence or a gesture with which your child can indicate to you that she is not going to answer.
- Teach your child that it is perfectly alright to say: 'That doesn't concern you' or 'I don't feel like talking about that now.'
- Make it clear to your child that she can share the simple truth if she wants to. For instance, she could say: 'Yes, I am adopted. That means that I have two families: my birth family lives in Brazil and the family who take care of me lives here. I live with the family who takes care of me, and they are my father and mother.' Or: 'My birth family lives in Russia. But I now live with my father and mother.'
- Try to practise or role-play difficult scenarios at home. By playing this out, your child can distance herself from the real setting. She will probably assign to you the role of the one who asks difficult questions and perhaps you both can have a good laugh about the play.
- Teach your child that she can tease and ask questions in return. One child will be teased because she has red hair and a big nose, another will be teased because she has brown skin. Every child can be teased about something. If a child asks: 'How did you get those stupid slit eyes?, ' your child could ask in return: 'How did you get that stupid gigantic white nose?'
- If your child is teased because you are not her real mother, teach her to ask in return: 'What does a real mother do for you?' Answers will probably include: 'She looks after me, is nice to me, makes sure that I am not hungry and am always safe. She is always there.' And then your child may say: 'My mother does all these things for me too, so I guess she is my real mother.'
- Explain to your child that children who tease are just waiting for an anxious reaction. If your child does not respond and apparently remains unaffected, the teaser will go away and look for somebody else to tease.

Conclusion

In this chapter, I have discussed how you can respond to questions and comments from your child and from outsiders. Many questions that are asked by adopted children are related to the grieving process that begins from about the age of seven. The last two chapters focus on this grieving process.

8

What is adoption-related grief?

Reading the signals

Children grieve when they are separated from their parents and from their familiar environment. For children who are adopted, this "acute grief" begins when the child is placed for adoption and continues until he is is safely bonded with his new parents and familiar with the new environment. Children show their grief by crying, laughing inappropriately, being angry or very withdrawn or fearful. It is often difficult for the new parents to recognise that these are signs of grief and to deal with them appropriately.

From about age seven, children become more aware that they have been relinquished by their birth parents. Their sadness is even more difficult to detect because adoption-related grief at this age is mostly not related to recent events. Additionally, children grieve intermittently; it suddenly stops and begins again, and this makes it hard for parents to read their child's signals accurately.

From about age seven or eight, adopted children often intermittently mourn and fantasise about "what could/should have been". Maybe they miss their brothers and sisters or grandparents who are still living in their birth country. As children do not understand that they actually are experiencing a grieving process, they will demonstrate this through their behaviour: they are more angry, confused, quiet or sad, or they experience physical disorders.

For many children, adoption-related grief is very difficult to cope with. Compared to other experiences of loss, there is no clear beginning and end to the process. Feelings of guilt, confusion and shame are added to the sadness of being relinquished. All these different feelings contribute to the child not having one specific and clear feeling about the loss of a person. It is complicated for young children to separate these different emotions. According to Brodzinsky (1992), adoption-related grief is complex because, on the one hand, there is a definite and seemingly final loss, but on the other hand, there is always hope for a reunion with the birth parents or other family members, if they are still alive. A child can become very confused if he tries to cope with these two extremes at the same time.

What do adopted children grieve for?

Adopted children can grieve for many different reasons. When and how intensely they grieve depends on their temperament and their personal adoption history (see later on in this chapter). When children are adopted at an older age, they will mostly grieve because they have been separated from their parents and their environment. They will also be sad about losing their language. Their new homeland can sometimes be so overwhelming that a child will only start speaking after a year. Babies and toddlers will grieve because they have lost routines as well as trusted sounds and smells, and the people who looked after them.

At a later stage, toddlers and young children often grieve because they look different from their adoptive parents; they would rather look like their father and mother and have grown in their mother's tummy. From about age seven, classmates become important to them and then they often feel sad because they look different from their friends. At the same time, they may also grieve about their name: some children mourn the loss of their original name, whilst other children would prefer to have a name that was easier to pronounce and less exotic.

Older children may also feel sad, confused or angry about what could/should have been. They may grieve about what happened to them and to their parents and siblings in their birth country, or worry about siblings who were adopted by other families.

During primary school, adopted children mostly grieve for the loss of their birth parents. According to Holly van Gulden and Lisa Bartels-Rabb, 'the child's focus is initially on the birth mother (rather than on both parents as a unit or on the birth father). Children are often curious about their birth fathers, but many will not ask questions or otherwise express their curiosity unless prompted' (2001, p. 198). According to these authors, young children don't often grieve for their birth fathers until they have worked through the sadness and anger related to losing their birth mothers. If children do grieve for the father, it is mostly in adolescence or in young adulthood.

Adopted children can grieve at various ages for the loss of:

- their birth parents
- their foster parents or their carers at the orphanage
- their family tree: the child is no longer linked to the generations
- their place in their original community
- their native country
- the culture of their birth country: smells, food, climate, religion, rituals and customs
- genetic and ethnic similarities to people around them
- their native language
- any siblings who stayed behind or were adopted by other families
- friends, special possessions, the house, the environment
- the children who stayed behind at the orphanage
- their original name

- their confidence that parents are strong and reliable and that they will always take care of their children no matter what happens
- their belief that most things in life are honest and just
- their right to determine their own fate/destiny
- their innocence: the accumulation of several losses may test their ability to trust in general
- their bodily integrity, if they were abused
  (Partly taken from *WAN-brochure* 'Verlies en rouw door adoptie', jaargang 4, no. 3, September 2001).

How do adopted children express their grief?

Children express their grief differently at various stages. Babies and very young children mostly show their grief by their body language, although extroverted, talkative toddlers may also be able to give words to their feelings. Most of them, however, express their grief by crying uncontrollably, by totally withdrawing into themselves or having no interest in play or food. Sometimes their behaviour is contradictory: on one hand, they want to sit on your lap, be hugged or picked up, but on the other hand, they protest and push you away. An adoptive mother writes about her 18-month-old toddler and how she experienced this:

> When our daughter had been with us for three months, we started holding her close to us in a baby carrier. The first few times she strongly protested, and then started to cry softly. After a few weeks her crying became more and more intense. We let her cry until she was finished, and then we comforted her by saying that she was sad and that we could understand why. One day, about three months later, I went to her room to wake her up. As soon as I came in she started to cry. She looked both very angry and very sad. She stretched her arms out towards me and I picked her up. She clung to me tightly and tried to push me away at the same time. She wept, wrapped her arms around my neck and scratched it. It looked like she wanted to say: 'I need you, Mum, and I

> want you to be with me, but I am so very angry about
> everything that has happened to me.'

Toddlers and young children can express their grief by regularly experiencing mood swings, being short tempered or by clinging to one of the parents. Other children sleep restlessly in the beginning, need nappies once again, show no interest in anything or experience physical disorders, for example, eczema. As a result of long periods of stress, children can also sweat profusely.

From about age six or seven, children can periodically become moody, depressed, confused, withdrawn or angry. They can also become jealous of their friends if they feel different or inferior. Some adoptees of this age are able to talk about their feelings if the adoption and the birth parents are frequently discussed subjects at home. Children are then better equipped to identify and recognise adoption-related emotions. Try to talk about the adoption often during this phase, answer your child's questions as well as you can and help him to understand what it means to be adopted.

Children who are grieving often display physical disorders. It is best to keep an eye on these disorders and to ascertain whether your child has one or more of the symptoms described below (taken from *Adoptietijdschrift*, theme nr. 'Verlies en rouw', jaargang 4, no. 3, September 2001). Possible physical symptoms are:

- stomach cramps, nausea or vomiting
- eating too much or too little
- irritated and sensitive bowels
- wetting the bed
- sleeplessness
- a dry mouth and difficulty swallowing
- joint and muscle pain
- headaches and migraine
- heart palpitations, dizziness, shortness of breath or even hyperventilation
- not growing

- often getting sick
- being lethargic/lacking energy or interest.

Nancy Verrier describes yet more possible physical symptoms (from the Dutch translation, 2003, p. 60):

- allergies
- asthma
- chronic tiredness
- problems with the immune system
- eczema or nettle rash
- stutter.

Possible psychological symptoms are:

- feeling sad
- longing vaguely for something
- feeling empty and incomplete
- feeling isolated
- frequently feeling anger, hopelessness, fear, resentment, shame or jealousy
- feeling guilty
- being anxious about rejection, separation, desertion, change
- having a negative self-image, tending to neglect oneself
- not being able to concentrate well at school and thereby experiencing learning difficulties
- displaying aggressive behaviour towards classmates
- often having intense dreams and/or nightmares
- being withdrawn or hyperactive
- asking for negative attention
- behaving provocatively
- being anxious about intimacy
- feeling depressed and having thoughts about suicide.

Most of these symptoms can occur at any moment and at any age, not only after a loss. If your child shows more than one of these symptoms, he is probably grieving about the adoption, although he may also be mourning other losses he has experienced. In every case, it is essential to take your child to see a doctor so that other causes not related to grief can be eliminated.

Circumstances/aspects that may influence adoption-related grief

Children do not all grieve in the same way. One will periodically be preoccupied with the adoption, another will treat it light-heartedly. Another child may not seem to be preoccupied with adoption, but is in fact thinking about it a great deal. Several factors will influence the intensity of each child's grieving process, for example, the temperament and gender of the child will partly determine how he handles the adoption-related loss. Boys tend to outwardly express their grief while girls tend to deal with it inwardly. The *physical and mental health* of a child (including the pre- and post-natal history), will also partly influence what a child feels about his adoption. Additionally, how much the child will allow himself to feel, will depend on the degree of basic trust and attachment to his adoptive parents. A child who has built up much basic trust and who is safely attached to his parents will be less anxious to feel sadness, anger and/or fear. Finally, *the adoption history* itself will influence the grieving process; some have experienced more intense losses than others.

It is best to always validate your child's emotions, whether they are sad or angry. Ultimately, he will have to deal with his losses and put his adoption into perspective; your child has to do this in his own way. Below are a number of variable circumstances that might determine the intensity of the grieving process and some guidance to help you to support your child through this grief.

Degree of attachment

If children do not feel safe enough, they often delay their grieving. Only very few children will show their sadness shortly after arrival.

They may show their feelings indirectly by having mood swings or sleep disturbances, or by being over-energetic or very quiet and withdrawn. Only when children are accustomed to their new situation and have bonded with their new parents will they feel safe enough to show their real feelings about the adoption and begin to trust.

If your child is at primary school, he will only show his real emotions when he feels safe enough and when he has developed enough basic trust. Only as a child begins to build his basic trust, will the suppressed emotions come to the surface. As a result, your child may show his emotions by having nightmares or by expressing fierce anger, extreme fear or sadness. The development of basic trust is essential for adopted children in order to cope with their experiences of loss. Nelleke Polderman writes about basic trust:

> Basic trust can be described as follows: the feeling that you can be who you are; that you never question whether your parents will stay, because you know that they *will* stay; the feeling that you are valued and that you won't lose yourself if, for example, you abide by other people's rules. That you won't lose your parents if you are disobedient. Children who have had a bad start, and that is the case with most adopted children, can lack basic trust to different degrees. This may be expressed by having concentration problems, behaving restlessly, not wanting to be touched or being too passive, too dominant or too competitive. It is important to children that they are being noticed and that they can be who they are.
> (Taken from 'Hechtingsproblemen tegenwoordig goed te behandelen', in *Adoptietijdschrift*, jaargang 5, no. 4, December 2002, pp. 21–23)

Nelleke Polderman identifies possible characteristic behaviours in a child who is not safely attached.

- He wants to be in control of everything.
- He wants to decide everything.
- He as difficulty sticking to the rules.
- He discourages physical contact.
- He withdraws from people or is indiscriminately friendly.

There is a better chance that your child will attach to you and develop more basic trust if you approach him with sensitivity and responsiveness (see Chapter 5). If your child has enough basic trust, he will in time be able to express his deeper feelings about his adoption; he will then feel safe enough to talk about his doubts and his possible loyalty conflicts. It is important that your child knows that he has your attention and that he may express his anger, his fears and his sadness. By naming your child's feelings, you show him that you have taken notice. 'You are sad', or 'You are angry because…' explicitly identifies his emotions (Step 1) and if you follow that by adding your opinion (Step 2), your child will get a sense of self-awareness and learn to recognise, understand and accept his own feelings. One adoptive mother writes about the effect that naming can have on your child's emotions:

> Michael (6) never really asked many questions about his adoption history, he really preferred not to hear anything about it. He also didn't want to go back to his birth country, not even on a holiday. Recently, he got a sister and he travelled with us to adopt her. He knew that his sister lived in an orphanage. We had explained to him earlier that some parents can't take care of their children because they have no money and can't buy food to eat. Suddenly he asked: 'Mum, what happens if you don't have money any more, will you send me away?' I tried to remain calm and stressed that he will always stay with us, no matter what happens. Then I went on talking about what really concerned him, namely the fear that we would desert him. At the end of the discussion I said: 'That is what you are scared of, that we do not want to take care of you any longer.'

Michael nodded his head, his lips trembled and he dived onto my lap. He started crying loudly. I comforted him for a long time and kept telling him that I understood his sadness and his fear, and that seemed to calm him down.

Adoptive parents' unresolved grief

Everyone experiences losses. The way in which you have dealt with losses in the past will indicate how you will deal with losses in the future. And your own experiences will determine how you handle your child's losses. If you have not come to terms with an important loss or if you have not grieved yourself, you might be frightened by the sadness and anger that your child feels, and you may even project your fear onto him.

If you experienced grief as a result of your involuntary childlessness, this may cloud your reaction. You may feel guilty because your intense wish for a child has resulted in your child being taken away from his trusted environment and now being unhappy. But those feelings of guilt are out of place, because your child would most probably have been adopted by another family if not by you. The fact that your child feels sad is not your fault (also see Chapter 1).

It will help if you overcome your own feelings of guilt and if you learn to recognise and accept your own defence or denial mechanisms before your child starts grieving about his adoption. Your child needs to come to terms with his anger and sadness and he needs to share his feelings with the people that are closest to him, and that is you. He can learn that his parents love him even if he is angry, sad or longing for "his other parents". By sharing his grief, you will strengthen his trust and the bond between you.

Presence of siblings

Siblings are able to share their memories. This can have a positive effect on learning to come to terms with the adoption, mainly because they can share and compare their memories with each other; they can check, correct and supplement what they each remember.

But the presence of siblings can also negatively affect the grieving process if their memories vary greatly. The older brothers or sisters often have a more complex history and may be more heavily defended in their emotions than their younger siblings.

Sisters and brothers arriving in new placements together can be very supportive of each other; they probably already have a relationship and may be able to speak their native language together. On the downside, there may be envy and rivalry because one may seem to attach more quickly and to get more positive attention from the new parents.

It is important that, from the beginning, parents approach each sibling in a sensitive and responsive way (see Chapter 5), so that all the children feel individually noticed and understood and get the same chance to attach safely in the short or long term. Parents should also try to give each child individual and exclusive attention that includes discussions about the past. This will enable each child to grieve in their own way.

Stability of the environment

If children grow up in a stable and open environment (family, school), they will probably feel safe enough to share their feelings with parents and teachers. They will also have the opportunity to put their feelings of loss into perspective.

But changes in the family or at school may affect the process of coming to terms with the adoption history. Adopted children are more sensitive to new losses and they can feel anxious or unsafe if someone close to them dies, if their adoptive parents get divorced, or if they have to move to a new house or another school. New losses may "pile up" on top of their not yet fully examined or worked-through adoption-related grief. An adopted child may therefore react to each new loss in an extreme way.

If your child is faced with an unexpected change or loss, try to offer as much structure and stability as possible to make up for it. Watch your child carefully. Try not to judge his behavior but instead identify it. During hectic days and weeks, try to find extra time to talk, walk, play or hug. If you feel that you yourself can't cope or that you can't get through to your child during a period of upheaval, seek advice from an adoption therapist.

Degree of support from the environment

Direct approaches from others around the child at school or in the community can also influence the process of coming to terms with the adoption. If teachers adequately deal with your child's adoption-related grief by talking about it in class (at your child's request or with his consent), or by discussing your child's adoption history with you and your child, he will probably feel understood and noticed. Grandparents, aunts and uncles, neighbours and good friends can also support your child. Try to mobilise this support over the years.

Nature and extent of the loss

The nature and the extent of the loss can greatly influence the intensity of the grieving process. Some children are so traumatised that they cannot even begin to grieve. Traumatised children may develop behaviour problems. Their losses can be so complex that neither they nor their adoptive parents can handle the situation adequately. In such cases, consult an expert. The sooner your child is able to work through his past, the sooner he will be able to get on with his life.

Phases of grief

Each adopted child will grieve in a unique way. One may react outwardly and intensely to the loss, while another may grieve inwardly and more slowly. One may feel the need to talk about it, while another may want to focus on his performance at school and prefer not to talk about it. Some children feel the pain of being relinquished but are then able to get over it quite quickly. Sometimes strong feelings of loss only come to the surface five, ten or even 20 years later.

What is common to each grieving process is not the time or the intensity, but the circle of emotions each child goes through. Elisabeth Kübler-Ross (1969) distinguishes between five stages of grief in adults as well as in children:

1. denial
2. reasoning/negotiating
3. anger
4. sadness/despair
5. detachment/understanding.

Below, each stage of adoption-related grief experienced by children is discussed in more detail (taken from 'Niet machtloos toezien', Rita Kobussen, Adoptietijdschrift, jaargang 4, no. 3, September 2001, pp. 32–35)

Denial

During the first phase, which usually occurs just after placement, young as well as older children may behave as if nothing has happened. They may carry on with their daily routine, perhaps imagining that the people they have left will reappear. This phase sometimes lasts for a few days, a few weeks, or even months. Some children sleep very deeply during this time, which may be a signal that, at night, the child is shutting himself off from his present situation.

At primary school age, a child can also go through this phase of denial. For example, he may continue to say that he has no problem with the fact that he is adopted. He may also be unresponsive or distant if his parents want to talk about his adoption. Or he may deny his adoption history by positively fantasising about his birth parents – this can happen if he is traumatised.

Denial can be very functional; as long as it isn't too extreme, it may work as a defence mechanism against overly intense feelings. Only when the child feels emotionally strong enough to face the reality and to feel the pain of the loss will he lower his defences. Sometimes a child isn't emotionally strong enough until he has reached puberty, or even later.

Reasoning/negotiating

At this stage, children often talk to themselves, God or the people from whom they are separated. Children often blame themselves for being "given away" and promise some imaginary friend that they will always be good if things can only be as they were before. If children are not yet able to negotiate verbally, they will act in an instinctive way by trying to change their behaviour. Some children may choose to be extremely good, while others decide to be naughty or angry; both types of behaviour result from the hope that they may then be allowed to go back to their birth country.

Anger

When the awareness grows that the situation is irreversible and the loss is final, children often start to feel angry. This can be expressed outwardly or inwardly. Outwardly, children can become disobedient or rebellious, experience mood swings, break things, kick, hit or bite. Inwardly, they may blame themselves for the loss and might think: 'My mother gave me away because I wasn't nice enough.' Children who are adopted between the ages of four and eight are often even more sensitive to feelings of guilt because they think "magically". If, before the adoption, they had thoughts like: 'I wish I had a new mother' or 'I wish my mother was dead', then they are likely to think that the death/separation from the parent(s) occurred because they wished it.

Sadness, despair

During this phase children are usually sad, tearful, irritable and sometimes uninterested in everything going on around them. They also may feel powerless, hopeless and full of shame, like in the phases before. They can be preoccupied with the question: 'Why did this happen to me?' They often don't eat or sleep very well. Your child might also stop growing for a while and become apathetic or sick. Some children regress to an earlier emotional stage and this may result in them feeling less connected to their peers for a while. Toddlers can suddenly behave like babies and young children like toddlers. When this phase is over, most children will return to their appropriate emotional level, but some may regress again at another time.

Detachment, understanding

In this final phase, children start to focus on the future again, although they may still experience feelings of sadness and/or anger every now and again. Upon arrival, young children will eventually detach themselves from their original caretakers and start focusing on the new caretakers. The younger your child is, the faster this will happen.

Children who are adopted at an older age will gradually make the transition from acute grief to more existential grief about their identity. Step by step they will understand that they were abandoned and that this is why they feel sad, angry or guilty. By working through this they can (possibly temporarily) come to terms with the loss.

Finally, children will integrate their loss into their sense of self. They will realise that they must get on with their lives without their birth parents or carers. They may cherish their memories as a way of staying connected to them.

Your child can reach this stage around age 11/12. He may go through the different stages of grieving again as a teenager or as an adult, especially if he wants to discover his roots, if he loses a special person or if he becomes a parent himself.

It is important to realise that these five stages of adoption-related grief often occur in a somewhat unstructured way. Most children will experience a tangle of emotions that is continuously shifting.

Conclusion

It is important to validate your child's grief. Try not to judge his feelings about his adoption. He must go through this grieving process in order to eventually find a physical and emotional balance.

Brodzinsky writes:

> Difficult as it is for parents to watch their adopted children try to deal with the pain of adoption-related loss, they can do nothing to spare them. They can, however, help ease the process by providing a supportive, nurturing environment in which the emotional storms of grieving can be weathered. When parents ask us what they can do to make this period

easier for their adopted children, we tell them to be available to their children, listen to them, help them clarify their emotions, and accept whatever feelings they are expressing. By their nonjudgemental responses, parents can show their children that these ups and downs are normal, real, acceptable – and temporary. (1992, p. 91)

In the following and final chapter you can read about how you can deal with adoption-related grief.

9

Dealing with adoption-related grief

Introduction

If adopted children feel safe in their new family, they will feel less afraid to show their emotions and talk about their past. The longer the child experiences this safe family connection, the greater the chance that she will develop well. It is not the case, however, that a safe attachment will lead to less adoption-related grief. The safer your child feels, the more intensely she may allow herself to be sad or angry about what happened to her. Below are suggestions on how to support your child and how to handle her adoption-related grief.

The importance of a safe, supportive environment

Children are not able to grieve entirely on their own. According to Deborah Gray, they need the unconditional support of their parents, as their parents are their source of comfort and emotional energy. Gray states that grief can be supported by providing the following:

- 'information about the loss
- assistance in reality testing (most children want to deny certain things)
- assistance in talking about their feelings
- help in determining what part they played in the loss (younger children are so egocentric that they are almost stuck here)
- permission and encouragement to share their feelings (possibly memories) about the person lost to them, and
- presence of a consistent adult, whom they trust, supporting their mourning.'
  (2002, p. 87)

It is not always easy for parents to offer so much unconditional support. One adoptive mother wrote about the sadness of her seven-year-old daughter Rose:

> Recently, my husband, Paul, was cross with Rose because she was being cheeky. She lay in her bed sobbing. We tried to sort out the argument with Paul, but then she said that she didn't feel at home with us. She said she wanted to be with her Filipino parents. I listened and she went on saying that she didn't feel right at school either or anywhere else, and that she sometimes just wanted to die when I was very angry with her. A day later we were in a supermarket together where she saw another adoptive family. Rose tugged at me and said: 'I would prefer to live with such a family.' We talked about it when we got home, and it affected me very deeply. This phase she is going through is having an enormous impact on me, although I know that Rose is grieving about her adoption. I sometimes can't respond to her properly because deep inside I feel so hurt. I am being rejected by my daughter, of course only to a certain extent, but nevertheless rejected. Yet I know my child has enormous trust in me because she dares to say those things.

Talking about the birth parents

If children grieve about their adoption, they are thinking about their birth family and what might have been.

- Who were my parents?
- Do I look like them?
- Why did they give me up for adoption?
- How was it possible that they couldn't take care of me any longer?
- Was it my fault that they sent me away, wasn't I good, nice or healthy enough?
- How could they just abandon me/take me to an orphanage when I was only a little baby?
- Why did they hurt me, abuse me, ignore me or neglect me?
- Why did they keep my (half)sister(s)/brother(s)?
- Why couldn't my parents get married?
- Couldn't they keep me secretly?
- Didn't I have a grandmother who could take care of me?
- Will I ever meet my parents, sisters, brothers?
- Why can't I stay in touch with them?

Curiosity about the birth parents is significant for developing a clear identity. Adopted children need to compare themselves with people who are important to them, and that includes the people who gave them their genes; the birth parents are part of their inherited characteristics and therefore their personality.

During periods of mourning, adopted children will feel the need to make connections between their birth parents and their own destiny. It is especially important to give children positive attention at this time. Nelleke Polderman writes:

> In order to give your child a feeling of security and safety, it is of the greatest importance that the child gets the feeling that his birth parents can be acknowledged in every respect. His birth parents are part of him.

Even if the child does not take the initiative, it is of the utmost importance that his parents often, and without pressure, talk about the birth parents. You can do this, for example, by commenting on whether he got his beautiful eyes from his birth father or birth mother. (2001, pp. 32–35)

Here is an example from an adoptive parent:

I commented on Jesse's (7) musical talent and told him that he must have got it from his African mother or father. He continued to tap his hands rhythmically to his favourite music. When the music stopped, I asked him if he ever thinks about his birth parents. He nodded and said: 'I often imagine that Mum is my Africa-Mum and that I live in Africa now and that you adopted me from America.' I asked him what he thought his Africa-mother looks like. Jesse answered: 'Long, very curly hair, dress, shoes and big earrings.' He asked me whether people in Africa wear big earrings and I said 'Yes'. Then he remembered the dimples in his cheeks. He said: 'If I write to my Africa-mother again, I will ask her if she also has nice dimples in her cheeks.' I said that I thought that was a good idea and that I would file that letter along with all the other letters he had written. Then Jesse said: 'I'll probably meet my Africa-mother if one day we go to Africa on a holiday.' I explained to him (as I've done before) that this is not certain and that we don't know how his birth parents are doing. Jesse sighed and said what fun it would be if his birth mother would come and visit him one day. I totally agreed and we imagined where she would sleep and what we would do.

Another adoptive parent writes:

Although I often go along with Yasmin's (6) fantasies

about her birth parents, I sometimes also try to guide these fantasies. I emphasise that a meeting with her birth parents will never be possible. And every time she asks 'Why not?' I repeat what I have told her before: 'People from China are only allowed to have one or two children because otherwise there will be too many people in China. Sometimes another child is born but Chinese families are not allowed to keep it.' I keep filling in more details at her pace. 'But I want to know what my China-Mum looks like', she says. I then tell her to look in the mirror because she probably looks like her birth mum. But she doesn't seem to get much out of this. She likes it, though, if we talk about her talent for gymnastics. We fantasise that maybe she inherited that talent from her Chinese father. She also makes friends very easily. Sometimes we imagine that this comes from her mother. The fact that her Chinese parents have passed things on to her that she can be proud of is noticeably doing her good.

It is important for adopted children to develop a positive image of their birth parents. Only then can they bond with those they have lost; only then can they actually start to grieve. In addition, a positive image of their birth parents will help to give adopted children a positive self-image, as they often strongly identify with their birth parents.

Eventually, adopted children should not only focus on the positive aspects of their birth parents, but also be aware of their negative characteristics, in order to build up a realistic impression. However, in order to work through their loss and form their own identity, children should never focus only on the negative aspects.

If children have experienced trauma before the adoption, and have a very negative impression of their birth parents, it is important for them to be able to express their anger and sadness about this. But they should also know that, despite everything, their birth parents wanted the best for their child. Your child probably thinks of her birth parents regularly, despite the fact that they abused or mistreated her. It is best to tell your child that her birth parents most probably hope that everything is going well with her. Your child has to learn that everyone has negative and positive characteristics, and that her parent's behaviour is not the same as her parent's identity. Only when your child can distinguish between these two things, can she create a positive image of her birth parents and start grieving.

Adoption-related grief after placement: a few points to consider

Grief experienced by adopted children soon after placement differs from the grief experienced from about the age of seven or eight. Children will experience greater shock reactions after arrival at their new home. They react more acutely to the loss of their caretaker(s), their trusted environment, the language, the culture, the climate, etc. Young, as well as older, adopted children have often been used to a very different way of life: maybe they were always allowed to play outside, got no attention whatsoever and learnt to accept that as the norm; perhaps they were treated very harshly or even beaten. These children may feel very unsure about how to cope with all the attention, kindness and love that they are now receiving from their new parents. Some children might always have lived in a crowded house surrounded by people, and they may be shocked by how quiet it is in their new home. If they were used to being looked after by many adults, it will be strange for them to have only one mother and father to rely on. Maybe they have never slept in a bed and therefore they find the mattress or bedstead very threatening; there is a chance that they may never have seen a staircase, and at first feel scared to go upstairs. Some children may be used to a tropical climate and therefore get cold when they first arrive in their new country. Others don't like the food or feel robbed of their native language.

Another difference with adoption-related grief experienced at a later stage is that, after arrival, children often are behind with their emotional and/or physical development; as a result, these children are often primarily focused on catching up and therefore are not yet able to grieve.

A third difference is that, in the beginning, children are not yet safely attached to the new parents and therefore the new parents first have to focus on building a safe bond with their child before the child can begin to mourn. This bonding process may be difficult, mainly because you don't speak each other's language yet and because the child sees you as the people who have taken her away from her own familiar environment. Sometimes it takes years before a child feels safe enough to show her parents her real feelings.

In the following paragraphs, you will find a few pointers that you can use to guide your child's grieving process after arriving at the new home.

It is important to know that not all apparent/distinct behaviour is a result of adoption-related grief. However, a discussion about different types of behaviour as a result of the adoption in general is not covered within the scope of this chapter.

Communication

- If you have videos or photos of your child's past, look at them together regularly. In the early days, this may reduce your child's feeling of homesickness or loss. If you feel that your child doesn't want to look at them, then put the videos or photos away for a while. Keep the important ones in a place where your child can find them and look at them by herself.
- Children don't often work through their emotions by talking about them. They connect to what they have experienced more easily through stories, by playing or by being creative. Read books together about adoption themes, create a personal adoption book, make up stories, let your child write a letter or a draw something for

their previous carers, or observe her while she plays (see Chapter 6). In this way, children can learn to recognise their feelings step by step and to eventually talk about their feelings and their memories. Children mostly work out for themselves what they think is a good way to cope with their grief. Teach your child that you accept her feelings of loss and that her sadness, as well as her gladness, about the adoption will be part of her life.

Attachment

- Most children only express their actual grief once they feel safe with their new parents. Especially during the first phase of bonding, it is important that you establish a good basis for your child in order to attach safely. Try to be there for your child as much as possible and try to react sensitively and responsively to her behaviour (see Chapter 5); by doing this she will learn that you are trustworthy, that you stay with her, that you notice her and that you are prepared to listen to her, even if she behaves negatively.
- Offering your child a structured daily routine with set times for eating and sleeping and recurring play and bath times will help her to attach to you more quickly and to feel safe enough to grieve.
- A safe bond will also be strengthened if you always respond in a clear and predictable manner. You can do this by calmly naming your child's behaviour or emotion (Step 1) and then expressing your own thoughts and feelings (Step 2).

However, staying calm and following these steps is not always easy for adoptive parents, particularly if your child cries continuously, totally withdraws, throws herself down on the floor and screams, or continually challenges you by very negative behaviour. As a result, you might feel the need to get angry, be irritated or be strict. However, it is best that you try to be as self-controlled as possible, especially at the beginning, because your child will perceive your strong emotion or irritation as unpredictable behaviour, and this might negatively affect the bonding process. Try to be aware of your anger before you express it, count to ten, take a deep breath and then deal with your child in the most soothing way possible.

Name/identify your child's behaviour and emotions objectively and give your own opinion. Tell her that her behaviour is not acceptable. Setting these boundaries will help your child to feel safe. After you have set the boundaries, you can give your child a positive perspective on the future. By remaining calm and by naming/identifying your child's behaviour step by step, she will eventually develop more basic trust and will most probably react in a less extreme way. You could say, for example:

> *You are very angry. I know you want to play outside with Lisa now that it's stopped raining. You have looked forward to it all afternoon. But I don't want you to play outside any more because we are going to eat soon. When we have finished eating, you can play outside with Lisa for a while.*

If your child doesn't listen and continues to shout at you, you could say:

> *You are angry because you would really like to play outside and that is why you are shouting at me. My ears are hurting. I understand that you are angry, but I want you to stop shouting right now.*

Repeat that message a few times if necessary. Stress that you want her to stop screaming and give her a choice: stop screaming or you go to bed early.

● If your child often reacts with anger, never shows her sadness, or if she is extremely withdrawn, you could try to make physical contact. You could let her sit on your lap for a while each day while you listen to music, play a game or read a book. You could also give her a massage just before she goes to bed. If physical contact is still too threatening for her, you could put a towel between her body and your hands. If you need advice you could ask someone who practises therapeutic massage. People who bottle up their anxiety may experience muscle pain; if the muscle tension is eased, your child may more readily express her emotions.

Physical contact can, in any case, be supportive during the time your child is developing basic trust and learning to express emotions. Maybe you can carry your baby or toddler in a baby-carrier during the first phase. If eye contact is still too threatening to your child, you could carry her with her face to the front.

If your child is still too scared to allow physical contact, try to "embrace her with your voice" as often as possible: make your voice soft and friendly, use nurturing words, and try to make and keep eye contact.

- Children often feel safer if they play and sleep in an enclosed area. Babies and toddlers may be more contented if they are wrapped up at night, play in a playpen or are held in a baby-carrier for some of the day; you could give slightly older children a hammock, a sleeping bag or a tent where they can be on their own for a while. If the playpen is too small for your child, you could also create a bigger play area that is closed off with a small gate.
- Before children can bond with the new parents, they need to have a physical and emotional balance. Some children need to regress to the time when they were a toddler or baby before they can attach and mourn. These children feel the need to emotionally catch up with a time when nobody met their basic needs, when they were never allowed to cry or disagree, or where they were left to cry unattended, or when they were never able to play with baby toys. Some children need a long period to attach safely to one parent before they can begin to attach to the other. Most children need two to three years to attach fully and to develop basic trust. Rememer that your child might only start to grieve once she feels completely safe with you.

Dealing with sadness and anger

- According to Aletha Solter (1998), children often express their emotions by crying, screaming or reacting angrily. Older children can also express their feelings through play and language. If a child cannot yet speak properly, it seems logical that she will express herself through strong emotions like crying and being angry. According to Solter, it is essential that children express their emotions. Only by doing this will they reach a physical and emotional balance. If a child is allowed to express her strong emotions (sometimes within limits), her extreme behaviour will (in most cases) eventually disappear. It can help to bear this in mind when your child is angry or sad. It is probably better to accept these strong emotions.

- If your baby or toddler cries a lot and seems inconsolable, she may be expressing her sadness about the separation, but she may also be crying because she is in pain or discomfort. If you are able to rule out all other causes and your child continues to cry, make sure that you offer her emotional safety by carrying or holding her as much as you can. Try not to suppress her sadness; let her cry for as long as she wants to. Talk to her reassuringly, and caress her if she allows you to. Show her that you accept her distress and that you are here for her. If your child does not want to be alone at night, let her sleep in your room or put a mattress down in her room so that one of her parents can stay with her. If your child is allowed to cry as much as she needs to, the intensity of her sadness will probably diminish.

- Don't ignore your child's moods. They might be an expression of grief. It is best to remain calm and not react angrily. At the beginning of your relationship she will benefit a lot if you show her that you notice her, that you don't reject her or turn your back on her, even if she is very badly behaved or angry. Bear in mind that your child has the right to negative as well as positive emotions. Sit with your child, place her on your lap (if she allows you to), acknowledge her emotions and behaviour, allow her to vent her grief. If necessary, set limits to her behaviour by saying, for instance, that she must not break things.

- Children can also release their feelings through humour. If you pretend, in play, that you are very angry or very sad, children may laugh uncontrollably.

Adoption-related grief from age seven onwards: a few pointers

Children in primary school express their sadness in a more subtle way. This is mostly due to the fact that they are older and not experiencing an immediate, direct loss. They gradually become aware of the fact that they were relinquished. As a result, a lot of adopted children will be faced with complicated and contradictory emotions, which they unconsciously will express through their behaviour. It will probably not be until age ten or 11 that they will be able to control these contradictory feelings. A mother writes about her seven-year-old adopted daughter and the difficulties that she experiences:

> Our daughter finds it difficult that she is adopted and that she looks different to the other children in her class. It makes her feel insecure and sometimes also sad and angry. It is difficult for her to grasp the fact that her birth mother loved her but couldn't take care of her. She would prefer to live in her birth country because the people there look like her. At the same time, she wants to stay here with us because she would miss us. She doesn't know which country she belongs to. These are very complicated thoughts for a child who is only seven years old.
>
> It makes us feel uncertain and anxious. At the moment she is clinging to us. She doesn't want to go to school, or play with her friends, or go to sleep unless we stay with her. My husband and I find it hard to watch. We can't take the pain away, she has to cope with the loss herself. On the other hand, we have noticed that the bond between us is growing stronger. Our girl certainly feels safe with us; she is very open about her thoughts and her emotions. That makes us the feel that we are on the right track.
> (From 'De Adoptieouder' (Drieluik-serie), from *Adoptietijdschrift*, no. 1, 2003)

As a result of their growing awareness about their adoption, children from about age seven or eight may suddenly become moody, depressed or confused. They might periodically vent their rage. They may defend themselves, unconsciously, from feeling the pain of loss by daydreaming or by becoming physically overactive. They could also become a perfectionist or start to concentrate obsessively on one thing (for example, they only want to watch television, to study or to become very good at one thing). Or they might start to behave very sociably and become very friendly. Although it may not look like this at first, this very sociable behaviour could be a defense mechanism. Possibly she is anxious that she will be rejected again if she expresses vulnerable or negative emotions.

Until a child is emotionally ready to face up to the truth, defense mechanisms can play an important and functional role. By using these, your child does not need to talk about her adoption and therefore she doesn't yet have to feel the existential pain of the loss. It is, however, important that you remain alert; if your child is showing defensive behaviour for long periods, she may be doing that out of fear. Children (and adults) are often scared to cry because sadness is a vulnerable emotion. If children are safely attached to their parents, they mostly show these emotions and allow themselves to feel the pain.

At this age (seven–12) it is not always easy to be sure of the difference between adoption-related behaviour and "normal behaviour" that is related to the child's temperament or to a particular situation at home. This is why adoptive parents have a difficult task: they must be aware of physical, psychological and behavioural symptoms that stem from adoption-related grief (see Chapter 8), but must also be careful not to interpret all behavioural problems as an indication that their child is grieving about her adoption.

Here are some pointers that you may be able to use if your adopted child uses defense mechanisms or shows signs of adoption-related grief.

Being aware of adoption-related emotions

- Solter (2002) talks about the "broken cookie phenomenon". Children sometimes allow their need to cry to build up until the urge for release is triggered if they get a broken biscuit instead of a whole one. These outbursts, which appear to be unjustified by the current situation, can be exasperating for parents. But it is often these little moments that trigger the built-up tears. Maybe your child wasn't feeling happy because something didn't go well at school, or maybe she had an argument with a friend at school. However, if these intense outbursts of emotions occur regularly after relatively insignificant incidents, it may mean that your child is using the pretext of small disappointments to release pent-up feelings of adoption-related grief.
- Watch out for shows of grief during celebration days related to the adoption. Perhaps your child is looking foward to her birthday, but on the actual day she is miserable, bad-tempered or doesn't even want to join in. These may be signs that your child is preoccupied with her origins and the relinquishment. Reassure her that you love her the way she is, even if she feels miserable or angry on her birthday. Later on, provide a safe place and time to listen to her and make her feel that she can always come and talk to you.
- Be aware that not all behavioural problems are adoption-related. All children, adopted or not, have moments or periods that they are not feeling very well; all children misbehave sometimes, want to withdraw, argue with friends, etc. However, if your child is behaving in a more extreme way than usual, there is always a chance that she is preoccupied with her adoption.

Communicating

- Make it clear to your child that she can always talk about herself, about her birth parents and her adoption, and about how she feels in this family.
- If your child asks a difficult or unexpected question at an inappropriate time, you could possibly say: 'That is a good question. Let us talk about it when we get home and then I will fetch the

documents (or, for example, the photos) as well.'

- Always tell the truth about your child's history. Try never to avoid her questions or to hold back information. Don't tell her everything at once, but rather provide her with a simplified version of what happened over time and gradually fill in more details. (See also Chapter 3.)
- If you don't know the truth, you could speculate. You could think of (realistic) "maybe's", for example:

> Your mother most probably didn't want you to go away, but she had no choice. I think that she really wanted to look after you because almost all mothers and fathers want to do that. Your mother probably thinks a lot about you and hopes that you are happy and healthy.

- During periods of grief you could make use of a life story book or an adoption book (see Chapter 6), or read stories with a related theme so that your child can identify with the main character.
- Be happy when your child asks questions about her adoption. It means that she feels safe with you and that she feels free to talk and think about it. Stimulate her curiosity and talk about it objectively, without judging the facts.
- Show understanding and validate her adoption-related feelings. Don't doubt your child's emotions, go along with her in this process. If your child is sad or angry about her adoption, don't try to change her opinion in this regard; your child has the right to feel the way she does. She will stop feeling sad or angry when she is ready to do so.

Dealing with evasive and defensive behaviour

- You may find it difficult to decide whether your child is in denial or if she has no need to grieve. An adoptive mother writes:

> I sometimes ask myself whether adopted children, by

definition, grieve about the loss of their birth parents. It is easy to identify the grieving process with our youngest daughter, Rose (7), who shows her adoption-related feelings in many different ways: she talks about her fears, her anger and her sadness. However, our eldest daughter, Jennifer (9), does not show her feelings in any obvious way. She says that she doesn't really think about her birth parents, and that we must stop assuming that she is sad about them. If Jennifer notices that Rose is sad about her adoption, she says it doesn't affect her. She only finds it sad for Rose that she feels like this. But if Rose cries because she has hurt herself, Jennifer is immediately by her side to take care of her little sister. Apparently Rose's physical pain does affect Jennifer.

If it seems that your child has no need to grieve, it may be that the adoption information is too painful to cope with; as a result, she may not yet be emotionally strong enough to deal with it. In this case, her defensive behaviour can be very functional. Her evasive or defensive behaviour may also indicate that your child has not yet built up enough basic trust and that she therefore is not yet ready to share her feelings. Your child may also have a flexible, strong character; in which case she is possibly able to handle difficulties more easily.

Whatever the reason for your child's defensive behaviour, always assure her that she can talk about the adoption and that she is allowed to love more than one set of parents. Observe your child closely, watch and listen to her while she plays, talks to friends, etc. Pay attention to non-verbal behaviour. Does she say "yes" in words but "no" with her body?

If your child is emotionally strong enough and if she seems to have sufficient basic trust and still isn't too fussed about the adoption, then she probably isn't deeply preoccupied with the pain of her loss at this particular time in her life.

- Regularly reassure your child that you value her as a person. Adopted children need this confirmation more often than birth children. Try to acknowledge this positive message to your child in different ways and as often as possible. You can do this, for example, by giving her many compliments and lots of personal attention.
- If your child says that she is not angry or sad, but at the same time behaves in a way that demonstrates that she is actually feeling very angry or sad, try to confront her in a friendly manner; perhaps she still will express her real emotions. An example:

  Maybe you aren't sad, but you look a little sad. I thought maybe you wanted to be hugged.

- You could also raise the subject of adoption indirectly by using the "pebbles technique" (see Chapter 5). Start with a one-liner that raises an issue and is then allowed to ripple until the child is ready to pick up on it. For example:

  If I were you, I would really like to know what my birth mother looks like.

  Can you see the moon? It is a full moon tonight. Maybe your birth mother is also looking at the moon tonight.

  You can play music so beautifully. I wonder who you got the musical talent from?

- Name/identify your child's defensive behaviour and ask her how you could help her. Children sometimes need some distance from their parents for a while in order to develop a more mature relationship with them. If necessary, give your child more freedom and allow her the space to find her own way.

Dealing with anger

- If you presume that your child is preoccupied with her adoption, try to accept your child's (perhaps intense) anger. Your child may hide her real feelings of sadness and shame behind stronger, defensive emotions like anger. Deep inside, adopted children often feel rejected and disappointed. Your child can only reveal her vulnerability if she is first given the opportunity to express her anger to you, both physically and/or verbally.

- Try to remain calm and not to get affected by your child's moods. Most parents experience difficulty in coping with anger because it is not a socially accepted emotion; it may be both alarming and threatening. Children may start kicking, hitting, shouting and throwing things. Parents often tend to react to this behaviour by becoming angry themselves, especially if they feel that they have lost control of the situation. Try to restrain your own feelings and talk calmly about the extreme behaviour so that your child does not get the negative confirmation that she is being difficult. Tell her that you understand her behaviour. Perhaps she is angry because she is scared or confused.

- It is preferable to not punish your angry child by sending her away (unless you have previously made an agreement in this regard, see below). Anger can also be used to show autonomy; adopted children may be testing how far they can go before they are rejected again. Sit next to your child if she is angry; it is better to name/identify her emotion in a neutral way than to tell her to stop. If she is punished by being sent to her room, she might interpret it as a personal rejection: 'You only love me if I behave nicely or if I am sad, but not if I am angry.'

- During intense, angry periods you should reassure your child even more frequently that you love her, that you value her dearly and that you will never leave her. Regularly remind her that she was not given up for adoption because there was anything wrong with her. Pay her compliments; say clearly what you like about her behaviour and how much it pleases you. Compliments make children feel more confident about themselves and can help them to behave in a more positive way.

- If your child expresses negative thoughts about her birth parents, do not confirm her opinion, however sad or painful her background is, because your child's anger may (at a later stage) be reversed and directed against you. Your child is struggling with her past; if you express negative thoughts about her birth parents, she may perceive this as negative information about herself. According to René Hoksbergen, it is better not to discuss negative thoughts about the birth parents or, if you do, only in a very subtle way (quoted in Delfos and Visscher, 2001, pp. 21–28).

- Teach your child that it is normal to have many different feelings about someone at the same time. She can love someone a lot and at the same time be very angry with that person. Remind her, for instance, that she was very angry with a friend recently, but that this child is, nevertheless, still her best friend. In this way, you can give your child the opportunity to have conflicting feelings about her birth parents and adoptive parents.
- If your child is by nature very energetic and/or combative, consider letting her join a martial arts class or participate in a sport in which she can regularly let off steam.
- Try, together, to find other ways in which your child can physically express her anger. Make an agreement about what is acceptable behaviour and what is not. For example, your child is allowed to slam a specific door very hard, to throw a ball against a wall or tree for a few minutes, to punch a boxing bag, to scream in the bathroom with the door closed, to jump on a trampoline, to run round and round the garden, to bite into a cushion, or to play an exciting computer game. If the list is clear and extensive, your child can decide how she needs to express her anger.
- Discuss and decide beforehand what the sanction will be if your child does not stick to the agreement. If she goes against the agreement and, for example, breaks something or hits other people, you can send her to "time-out". In this case, her behaviour will have had consequences.
- If your child expresses her anger in an acceptable way, you should compliment her so that she learns that she may be angry, but that she must stick to the agreement because not all ways of expressing anger are acceptable.
- Be aware of your own behaviour. If you get angry and break something or slam a door, your child will find you untrustworthy and will probably not stick to any agreement you made together.

If you behave in an unacceptable way, it is best to apologise immediately and acknowledge that you should have reacted differently.

- Perhaps your child only shows her anger when she is at home. This probably is a result of the fact that she feels safe with you. If your child behaves extremely destructively or is anti-social or withdrawn/depressed, ask for advice from an adoption therapist. Perhaps your child does not (yet) have enough basic trust, or maybe she is preoccupied with her adoption.

Dealing with sadness and fear

- Crying can have therapeutic value, especially in situations involving loss. According to Aletha Solter (1998), crying is a necessary part of the grieving and recovery process: if your child is able to show her sadness openly by crying, it will help her to cope with the stress and to recover more quickly physically and emotionally.
- If your child is sad about the loss/separation, she is vulnerable. Ensure that she feels emotionally safe with you. You will probably help her most by validating her sadness and by giving her a shoulder to cry on. One adoptive mother writes:

> I put my son Ivan (8) to bed. We had had a wonderful day together and we chatted about all kinds of things. I wanted to kiss him goodnight but then he suddenly put his arms around my neck and whispered: 'Mum, I cried last night when I was in bed.' 'Why did you cry, sweetie?' I asked. 'I cried because I was thinking about my real mother. That is where I want to be.' His tears started running down my neck. He was intensely sad. I couldn't do anything except be there and hold him tightly.

Try not to suppress or reduce your child's sadness by making positive comments. If your child can openly talk about her grief or fear, she will most probably be able to work through the grief herself.

- Children often work through their grief through stories, fantasies or play. This can give some structure to their emotional reality. You could read books together that relate to the specific fear or emotion your child is experiencing. The theme of a book might focus on the loss of someone you love, or on loneliness, separation, running away, being forgotten, being lost and found again, being rescued or being celebrated. It can help your child if she can identify with the main character in a story. Your child may also express her grief by making drawings, writing letters, etc (see Chapter 6).
- Humour can be a good healing mechanism: pretend-play that you are a scared, lost or lonely child. There is a good chance that your child relates to the story from a distance and maybe she wants to take on the role of the comforting, strong father or mother or sister or doctor which she might do with an exaggerated playfulness. A good laugh about something often releases the tension.
- One of the biggest fears of adopted children is that they will be abandoned again by their loved ones. From your child's perspective, this fear of separation is very realistic. An adoptive mother writes about her six-year-old son Richard and his fears:

> Richard (6) always finds it very difficult to say goodbye, either at the school gates or when going to bed at night. One evening, after a difficult day at school, I took him to bed and he told me that he always feels horrible at school or when he is alone in his bed. He said: 'I feel so terrible because I think about you and you are not there and then I am scared that you won't come back.' We spoke a little about his fears and then he said: 'I really, really don't like this feeling, Mum, I don't want to feel like that.' I told him that I could very well understand him. Then he suddenly said: 'I know why I feel like that, Mum; it is because I wasn't in your tummy.' I was very touched when he said that and told him that it was well thought through and that, yes, his feelings would have been different if he had grown in my tummy. I also reassured him that I was very happy that he came to live with us, that he is my child forever,

> **that I will never leave him and that I will always take very good care of him.**

- If your child is often fearful of being left alone, try to build up her basic trust. Approach her in a sensitive and responsive way, as often as possible. Your child might eventually get over her fear. Accept her fear and try not to set a deadline for when she should get over it.
- When your child is grieving, her cognitive, emotional and physical development may temporarily slow down. She might not grow as much, her co-ordination may suffer or she may not do as well at school as her classmates. If she can put her grief into perspective or learn to cope with it, she will probably catch up eventually.
- For a period, your child may behave as if emotionally younger than her actual age or she may be more clingy to you than normal. This could indicate that she should be treated at a different emotional level. Her behaviour will most probably normalise once she begins to understand a bit more about her adoption.
- If your child is inclined to withdraw when she is grieving, you could buy her hoodies or jumpers with very long sleeves so that she can cover her head or her hands when she is feeling insecure. Make sure that she has her favourite lunch and drink to take to school every day, so that she is sure that she has everything she needs. If she likes, include her favourite game, a cuddly toy or a photo. Let her wear clothes that she feels comfortable in and buy her an amulet to "protect" her that she can keep with her all the time. Reassure her that she is doing well and don't expect too many achievements at school. Tell the teacher that your child is feeling vulnerable and explain the situation, without giving away your child's private details.
- Keep in touch with the teacher and let him or her know that it would be better not to discuss adoption-related issues in class for the time being. Explain that your child is currently very sensitive and that you don't know how long this period will last. It may be over next week or it may last a few months or even a year. Your child will feel safest in a group where, in terms of her adoption, nothing is forced and she isn't exposed in any way. Ask the teacher if he or her will monitor her vulnerability and treat her with consideration in the group; she may prefer to stay in the background for a while.

- Here is an example of a structured dialogue that you can use when talking to your child about her adoption-related grief:
  1. Give a confirmation of receipt so that you can find out what your child meant (Step 1).
  2. Say that you understand that your child feels this way/validate her words (Step 2). Don't diminish or deny anything. Sometimes it is best to stop the dialogue after this confirmation. Your child is now able to take the time to feel the pain. Depending on the situation, you can continue with the discussion.
  3. Tell her what the situation is or was. You could possibly say something positive about the birth parents or about another fact of the adoption.
  4. If necessary, provide positive options for the near future or for later on.

- If you feel that you can't guide and support your child when she needs to grieve because the situation is, for some reason, too complicated, consult an adoption therapist. She or he can probably help you to help your child to get through the grieving process.

Conclusion

- If your child continuously feels sad or angry about her adoption and you feel that she has "got stuck", then don't carry on talking about it too much. Rewarding, punishing and ignoring are all forms of attention and can be experienced as rewarding. Name/identify your child's emotion (Step 1), give your opinion (Step 2) and then put the subject to rest.
- Be careful that you don't interpret all your child's distressing behaviour as adoption-related. Difficult behaviour can also be caused by difficult daily situations: there may, for example, be problems at school. It is easy to become so used to thinking in terms of adoption-related behaviour that you seldom interpret your child's behaviour as a result of any other reason or situation. What is important is to be able to distinguish between the two.

Afterword

When I began to write this book, my ideas were, of course not, yet clearly formulated. Early on, I knew that this had to become a concise, practical book. I thought that I would be able to cover the essence of this subject in seventy or eighty pages. But the more research I did, the more I realised that this was impossible, and it is now a substantial handbook.

The risk in writing such a specialised book about raising adopted children is that the reader might get the feeling that adopting children from overseas is a task that is almost impossible to accomplish. The underlying message of my book may contribute to this: adopted children are vulnerable and the development of their personality also depends on how you handle their adoption history.

While reading this book, you may have begun to doubt your own strategy in raising your child while, in your eyes, you were doing very well until now. I would really like to emphasise here that there is no "best way" to bring up adopted children. In most cases you are probably reacting adequately and responding intuitively to your child in a way that is good for him or her. The purpose of my book is to offer ideas for the times when intuition lets you down, and when you are not sure how to handle your child's adoption history.

Besides, it may be good to realise that almost all of us doubt our parenting strategies at some point. Raising any child, adopted or not, is a complex task. What is most important is that you are prepared to look at yourself and your child, and that you learn to understand what does and what does not work out well and why that is the case. The basis of your bond of trust is established by the fact that you take care of your child on a daily basis and that for most of the time you are attuned to your child's behaviour. At the same time, your child will learn from the experience that his parents also make mistakes sometimes, and that nobody is perfect, not even the people he loves the most. Revealing your own imperfections can help your child in his own development and in his future expectations of other people.

After reading this book, you may tend to interpret your child's behaviour as stemming from her adoption history. It can do no harm to be aware that different behaviour may stem from her adoption. At the same time, it is nevertheless important to see your child as a "normal child" with a genetic make-up and a temperament that she was born with. One child may be introverted and feel the adoption-related pain for a long time; another child may be more extroverted and deal with her past more easily. One will use humour or play to deal with her grief; another will prefer to be left alone. If you would like to find out more about your child's temperament, you could read *Nurture by Nature* (see Useful Reading). In this book, 16 different types of children are described. It offers insight into the strengths and weaknesses of different kinds of children and teaches parents what they should and should not expect from their children. Reading this book taught me to look at my children without continuously considering their adoption histories.

In conclusion, I would like to say one more thing: adopted children (just like normal children) need space to learn to fly during each phase of their life. If you have met most of their needs, including the "adoption needs", then it is important that your child also learns to function independently and that he learns that he won't always need his parents to enable him to cope. If you encourage his efforts to be independent at every stage of his development, you will equip him with the self-confidence to step into adulthood.

Bibliography

Adoptietijdschrift (2001) 'Verlies en rouw' ('Loss and grief')
Adoptietijdschrift, number 3, September
(*An independent magazine for all those involved in adoption.*)

Brodzinsky D (1992) *Being Adopted: The lifelong search for self*,
New York, NY: Double Day

Delfos M F (2002) *Luister je wel naar mij? Gespreksvoering met
kinderen tussen vier en twaalf jaar*, Amsterdam: SWP (English
edition: (2001) *Are you listening to me? Communicating with
children from four to twelve years*, Amsterdam: SWP

Delfos M F and Visscher N (ed) (2001) *(Pleeg)kinderen en vreemd
gedrag?! In 13 thema's*, Amsterdam: SWP

Gray D (2002) *Attaching in Adoption: Practical tools for today's
parents*, Indianapolis, IN: Perspectives Press

Gulden H and Bartels-Rabb L (2001) *Real Parents, Real Children*,
New York, NY: Crossroad

Hoekema E (2002) *Verlies en rouw door adoptie: informatie voor ouders*, Utrecht: Stichting Adoptievoorzieningen

Juffer F (1999) *Adoptiekinderen, opvoeding en gehechtheid in het gezin*, Amsterdam: Boom

Keefer B and Schooler J (2000) *Telling the Truth to your Adopted or Foster Child*, Westport, CO: Bergin & Garvey

Kohnstamm R (2002) *Kleine ontwikkelingspsychologie I*, Houten/Diegem: Bohn Stafleu Van Loghum

Melina, L R (2001) *Making Sense of Adoption: A parent's guide*, New York, NY: Harper Collins

O'Malley B (2002) *Lifebooks: Creating a treasure for the adopted child*, Winthrop, MA: Adoption-Works

Polderman N (1998) 'Hechtingsstoornis, beginnen bij het begin', *Tijdschrift voor Orthopedagogiek*, number 10, pp. 422–433

Polderman N (2001) 'Vaste grond onder de voeten – kinderen zonder bodem bestaan niet', *Wereldkinderen*, jaargang 27, nr. 2/3, May

Polderman N (2003) 'Basisvertrouwen opbouwen na een slechte start', *Wereldkinderen*, jaargang 29, nr. 1, February

Polderman N (2003) 'Hechtingsproblemen tegenwoordig goed te behandelen', *Adoptietijdschrift*, jaargang 5, nr 4, December

Polderman N (2008) 'Kinderen zonder "bodem" bestaan niet. Hechting en Video interactie Begeleiding', accessed at www.basictrust.com

Polderman N / Basic Trust (2002) *Toelichting op enkele interactieprincipes van de Video Interactie Begeleiding*, Amsterdam: Basic Trust

Solter, A (1998) *Tears and Tantrums: What to do when babies and children cry*, California, CA: Shining Star Press

Verrier N (2003) *Afgestaan, Begrip voor het geadopteerde kind*, Amsterdam: Ambo. Dutch translation from (1993) The Primal Wound, New York, NY: Gateway Press

Viorst J (1987) *Necessary Losses*, New York, NY: Simon and Schuster

Watkins M and Fisher S (1993) *Talking with Young Children about Adoption*, London: Yale University Press

Useful books

BAAF publications are listed on our website at **www.baaf.org.uk** and can be purchased there or by phone on 020 7421 2604. BAAF also maintains an email contact list for updates and new publications: to subscribe to this please visit www.baaf.org.uk.

Books for adopted children and young people

Camis J, **My Life and Me**, BAAF, 2001
This life story book includes space for drawings, photographs, documents and a record of thoughts and feelings at various stages in the child's life. It is designed to be completed by children, with help and support from appropriate adults; practice guidelines provide help for those undertaking direct work.

Children's guide series, BAAF
This series of children's guides provides simple and easily understood explanations of adoption and various other subjects.

Shah S, **Adoption: What it is and what it means**, BAAF, 2003
Designed to appeal to children and hold their interest, this booklet provides a good introduction to adoption, the process and

procedures, with easy to understand definitions. Colourful, vividly illustrated and presented in accessible and jargon-free language.

Shah S and Argent H, **Life Story Work: What it is and what it means**, BAAF, 2006
A colourful children's guide for children who are embarking on life story work or are already doing it, with simple explanations of what is a complex activity.

Foxon J, **Nutmeg Gets Adopted**, **Nutmeg Gets Cross**, **Nutmeg Gets a Letter, Nutmeg Gets a Little Help, Nutmeg Gets into Trouble**, and **Nutmeg Gets a Little Sister**, BAAF, 2001, 2002, 2003, 2004, 2006 and 2007
This series of books for children about Nutmeg the squirrel and his adoptive family offer a practical way to explore and understand some of the situations and feelings that can be linked to adoption. Subjects covered include painful memories, feelings of anger and confusion, and contact issues.

Argent H, **Josh and Jaz have Three Mums**, BAAF, 2007
An illustrated story for children aged four to ten looking at the subject of lesbian adoption and, more generally, diversity in family structures.

Griffith J, **Picnic in the Park**, BAAF, 2007
A picture book for young children which, through the story of a birthday picnic in the park, looks at how families can come in all shapes and sizes.

Seeney J, **Morris and the Bundle of Worries**, BAAF, 2007
An illustrated story for children aged four to ten, looking at worries and how, through talking about them with other people, these can be lessened or become more manageable.

Bell M, **Elfa and the Box of Memories**, BAAF, 2008
An illustrated story for children aged four to ten, which discusses the importance of memories and how sharing them and

remembering the good times is better than keeping them locked away.

My Life Story CD-ROM, Information Plus, 2003
This CD-ROM will guide worker and child through a range of life story activities to assemble key information, process current situations and consider what the future might hold. Music, sound effects, colour animation and attractive graphics add to the appeal.

Bond M, **The Paddington Books**, Collins
These books are well known to most children but remember that Paddington has to get used to living in a family for the first time. He has brought with him from Peru his scrapbook, a photo of his Aunt Lucy, and little else. He settles down in his new home despite many traumatic experiences but often thinks back to his past.

Miller K A, **Did My First Mother Love Me?**, Morning Glory Press, 1994, USA
A story for an adopted child with a special section for adoptive parents. In the story Moyan has a letter from her birth mother which she needs to read with her adoptive mother; she then wonders: did my first mother love me?

Plumtree D, **Helping Children to Build Self-Esteem**, Jessica Kingsley, 2001
This book was produced for a range of people who work with young children to help them develop. A number of the activities are easily adaptable for use on an individual basis with adopted children.

Striker S and Kimmel E, **The Anti-Colouring Book**, Scholastic, 1986
This interactive book for children aged five to ten contains a wide range of suggestions to stretch a child's imagination. Each page gives a hint of a picture and a sentence at the bottom to get started.

Keep a note of books that your child may have found useful during preparation so that you can locate these again if needed.

Letterbox Library has a wide variety of titles for children, covering many different family structures and diversity issues – call 020 7503 4801 or visit www.letterboxlibrary.com. The book reviews published in *Adoption & Fostering*, BAAF's quarterly journal, and *Adoption Today*, the monthly magazine from Adoption UK, can also provide ideas of useful titles.

A range of books have been designed to help children put together information about themselves and their family, which can help build self-confidence. *The Anti-Colouring Book* and *Helping Children to Build Self-Esteem*, listed above, are good examples. Some need careful screening in advance if they contain assumptions about families which are difficult for your child.

Novels for teenagers

Blackman M, **Hacker**, Corgi, 1992
At the beginning of this book Vicki, adopted as a baby, isn't exactly best pals with her brother who was born into the family! But when her adoptive father is arrested and accused of stealing over a million pounds from the bank, she is thrust into an adventure with her brother trying to prove her father's innocence. The ending not only solves the crime but it also establishes the relationship between Vicki and her brother and how she belongs in the family.

Leach B, **Anna Who?**, Attic Press, 1994, Eire
Anna's adopted. When she was little her mother used to call her "our special daughter". But now Anna is 14 and she doesn't feel so special anymore. All Anna wants to do is to get away from her family and discover who she really is. But then something happens and Anna slowly begins to realise that she doesn't need to know where she came from to know who she is.

Lowry L, **Find a Stranger, Say Goodbye**, Viking Kestrel Books, 1980

The story of an adopted girl's search for her birth mother. Everything is going well in her present family but she needs to know her background. She carries out her searching in a responsible way and the feelings it stirs up are realistic. Eventually she finds her birth mother and returns to her adoptive family who she discovers to be her "real" parents.

Nerlove E, **Who is David?** Child Welfare League of America Inc, 1985, USA

An involving story that should capture the attention of many adopted adolescents, especially boys. David struggles with his curiosity about his original parents in a happy adoptive home. His emerging friendship with Diana is sensitively described.

Note: Children's books are regularly reviewed in *Adoption Today*, the newsletter published by Adoption UK.

Books for parents and carers

PARENTING

Archer C, **First Steps in Parenting the Child who Hurts**, Jessica Kingsley, 1999

This book offers practical, sensitive guidance through the areas of separation, loss and trauma in early childhood. Archer sets out to encourage confidence, confessing this is the book she herself (as an adoptive parent) would have welcomed 20 years ago.

Archer C, **Next Steps in Parenting the Child who Hurts**, Jessica Kingsley, 1999

This volume follows on from the First Steps book, continuing the challenging journey through childhood and into adolescence, explaining the effects of early emotional trauma and reviewing specific sensitive situations that commonly arise.

Argent H, **Related by Adoption**, BAAF, 2004
Grandparents and other relatives who become related by adoption
can play an invaluable role in the life of the adopted child. This
handbook gives an introduction to adoption today and discusses
how the wider family can provide support.

Cairns K, **Attachment, Trauma and Resilience**, BAAF, 2002
One of BAAF's bestselling titles, this compelling book draws on
the author's professional and personal experience of 25 years of
fostering to explore how her family responded to the children's
difficult feelings and behaviour. Suggestions for how to help
promote recovery and develop resilience are woven throughout the
story.

Finding a Way Through, (video), Kate Cairns in conversation with
John Simmonds, BAAF, 2003
John Simmonds, Director of Policy, Research and Development at
BAAF, talks to Kate Cairns, author of *Attachment, Trauma and
Resilience*, about her experiences of being a parent/carer on this 60
minute video, an essential supplement to Kate's highly regarded
book.

Hicks S and McDermott J, **Lesbian and Gay Fostering and
Adoption**, Jessica Kingsley, 1998
This immensely readable book will be of enormous encouragement
to lesbians or gay men who foster or adopt, or are considering
doing so. It tells openly and honestly how it is without becoming
weighted down with politics or jargon.

Howe D, **Adopters on Adoption**, BAAF, 1996
This absorbing collection of personal stories from experienced
adopters whose children are now young adults describes the
importance and distinctiveness of adoptive parenting. An essential
read for adopters and adoptive people.

The Our Story Series, BAAF
This series of real-life adoption memoirs, written by adopters, looks at a variety of adoption scenarios and experiences.

James M, **An Adoption Diary**, BAAF, 2006
An inspiring real life narrative of one couple's journey to adoptive parenthood, which talks openly and honestly about the adoption process.

Seymour N, **In Black and White**, BAAF, 2007
An honest account describing a white couple's adoption of two black children, over a 20 year period. The story follows the children through contact with their birth family and the effect this has on their lives.

Wise J, **Flying Solo**, BAAF, 2007
A humorous and heart-warming personal story which follows the author as she adopts a child on her own; this book describes the realities of life for single adopters.

Carr K, **Adoption Undone**, BAAF, 2007
The true story of an adoption breakdown, bravely told by the adoptive mother. From the final court hearing, when Lucy returned to local authority care, Karen Carr looks back over the four years Lucy was with them and, without apportioning blame, describes what went wrong and why.

Royce R and Royce E, **Together in Time**, BAAF, 2008
An open and honest account of how creative music and art therapies helped a family who adopted two boys with attachment difficulties.

Marsden R, **The Family Business**, BAAF, 2008
Narrated by the adoptive father, this is an honest account of adopting a child with a disability and the impact on the whole family. It explores the challenges of day-to-day life and the

importance of focusing on the child's personality rather than his disability.

Phillips ZH, **Mother Me**, BAAF, 2008
A frank and honest personal memoir which explores the far-reaching impact of adoption on childhood, adolescence, relationships and self-esteem. It also provides a unique insight into pregnancy and motherhood from the perspective of an adopted woman.

Mulholland J, **Special and Odd**, BAAF, 2007
A revealing and extraordinarily witty memoir which tells the story of how the author met his birth mother 29 years after being given up for adoption.

Morris A, **The Adoption Experience**, Jessica Kingsley, 1999
Actual adopters tell it like it is at every stage of the adoption process, from the moment of first deciding to adopt to feelings about children seeking a reunion with birth family members, or simply leaving home.

Salter A, **The Adopter's Handbook**, BAAF, 2006
The first of its kind, this guide aims to help adopters help themselves through the adoption process and beyond. Information is included on processes, legal issues, education and health, needs of the child and parent, and post-adoption support.

Van Gulden H and Bartels-Rabb L, **Real Parents, Real Children**, Crossroads, 1995
This book takes parents and professionals through the stages of child development, explaining what adopted children at each age commonly think and feel about adoption and how parents can respond.

ADOPTION SUPPORT

Phillips R and McWilliam E, **After Adoption: Working with adoptive families**, BAAF, 1996
This unique anthology, illustrated with case studies, focuses on post-adoption support for adoptive families.

SEARCHING AND REUNION

Feast J, Marwood M, Seabrooks S, Webb L, **Preparing For Reunion, The Children's Society**, 1998
Adopted people, adoptive parents and birth parents tell their stories. This book addresses many of the commonly asked questions like, when should I search? What am I letting myself in for? Am I being disloyal? Should I keep this secret? Do I really need counselling?

Howe D and Feast J, **Adoption, Search and Reunion**, BAAF, 2004
This fascinating study compares a group of adopted people who searched for birth relatives with a group who did not, looking in detail at the factors that influenced their decisions. The extensive quotes from adopted people provide an absorbing read.

USEFUL GUIDES

Barn R, **Working with Black Children and Adolescents in Need**, BAAF, 1999
This book aims to help develop an overall understanding of "race" and culture. Themes tackled include strengthening racial identity, developing anti-discriminatory practice and meeting the needs of transracially adopted black children.

Douglas A and Philpot T, **Adoption: Changing families, changing times**, Routledge, 2002
Drawing together contributions from adopted people, birth parents, adoptive parents and practitioners, this anthology provides unique

insights into the subject of adoption and exposes some of the myths surrounding it.

Keefer B and Schooler J, **Telling the Truth to your Adopted or Foster Child**, Greenwood, 2000
A collection of practical guidelines and tools to help parents communicate with their children about the circumstances of their past.

Nicholls E, **The New Life Work Model**, Russell House, 2005
A practice guide looking at how to make life story work more effective, and broadening its focus from immediate to lifelong needs.

Ryan T and Walker R, **Life Story Work**, BAAF, 2007
An invaluable guide to the innovative and imaginative techniques now available to help children come to terms with their painful pasts. It outlines the background theory and offers practical suggestions for using games and projects like family trees, maps and life graphs that aid the healing process. Illustrated with drawings and photographs.

OTHER BOOKS

Surviving Five, Barnardo's, 1993
This short, very readable book gives an insight into how one family coped with the different needs of a family of five brothers and sisters from introductions through the first year of placement. It shows some of the issues that need to be addressed with children at different ages and stages.

Bernstein A C, **Flight of the Stork: What children think (and when) about sex and family building**, Perspectives Press, 1994, USA
An expansion of an earlier book on talking to children about sex, recognising their needs and what they understand at different

stages of development. The new edition includes chapters on children born as a result of assisted reproduction and those growing up in adoptive and stepfamilies.

Buchanan E, **From China With Love: A long road to motherhood**, Chichester: John Wiley & Sons, 2005
A frank and honest personal memoir about adopting a child from China.

Howe D, Sawbridge P, Hinings D, **Half a Million Women, The Post-Adoption Centre**, 1997
This book examines aspects of the experience of giving up a child for adoption.

Jones M, **Everything you Need to Know about Adoption**, Sheldon House (SPCK), 1987
A very useful guide to adoption with plenty of quotations from people who've "done it". Includes material on transracial and intercountry adoption.

Kay J, **The Adoption Papers**, Bloodaxe Books, 1991
Jackie Kay was adopted transracially by a white Scottish couple. This collection of poetry expresses the different viewpoints of the mother, birth mother, and daughter.

Harris P (ed), **In Search of Belonging**, BAAF, 2006
An anthology of writings, memoirs, poetry and artwork by transracially adopted people from countries as different as Kenya, Hong Kong, Cambodia and Sri Lanka.

Harris P (ed), **The Colours in Me**, BAAF, 2008
An anthology of writings, poetry and artwork by adopted children and young people, about their adoption, their feelings and their experiences.

Bishoff T and Rankin J (eds), **Seeds from a Silent Tree**, Pandal Press, 1997

An anthology of thoughts, writings and memoirs by transracially adopted people from Korea, looking at their experiences of adoption and feelings about their identity.

Krementz J, **How it Feels to be Adopted**, Orion, 1984
The views of 19 adopted young people in the USA, ranging in age from 8 to 16 years old. It could be read by adults or children and reflects many of the feelings children have about their adoption.

Post-Adoption Centre, **A Glimpse through the Looking Glass**, 1990
A discussion paper that examines issues of relevance to transracially adopted black adults.

Rosenberg E B, **The Adoption Life Cycle**, The Free Press, 1992
A readable book which combines current research theory and practical advice relevant to all those directly involved in the adoption experience – adopters, adoptive parents and birth parents, as well as professionals. It provides a framework for understanding the important developmental tasks which span the lifetimes of those involved.

Ruskai Melina L, **Making Sense of Adoption**, Harper & Row, 1989
This book includes advice and many examples of age-specific activities to help answer questions like - How do I share information that might upset my child? How can I know when my child is wondering about adoption?

Thomas C and Beckford B with Lowe N and Murch M, **Adopted Children Speaking**, BAAF, 1999
This book is full of poignant testimonies offering revealing insights into what children and young people think about adoption. Themes covered include beginning the process; matching and introductions; contact; and adoptive home and school.

Tugendhat J, **The Adoption Triangle**, Bloomsbury, 1992
What happens when adopted people wish to search for their lost

families? This book includes interviews with many adopted adults, birth parents, and adoptive parents and those professionally involved. Starting from looking at the particular perspectives of birth mother, birth father, adopted individual and adoptive parents, it goes on to explore both the search and reunions.

Verrier N, **The Primal Wound**, Gateway, 1996
This is an in-depth exploration of pre- and perinatal psychology, attachment, bonding and loss, and explores the effects on adopted children of separation from the birth mother.

Wells S, **Within me, Without me**, Scarlet Press, 1994
This collection of personal stories explores the experiences of mothers who have given up children for adoption.

Note: Books for adults are regularly reviewed in *Adoption & Fostering*, BAAF's journal and in *Adoption Today*, the newsletter published by Adoption UK.

Leaflets from BAAF – Advice Note series

If you are Adopted
Answers to some of the questions adopted children ask, aimed at the children themselves. Includes information on tracing birth parents.

Talking about Origins
An outline of adopted children's need to be told about adoption and the law on access to birth certificates and information.

For further reading

Articles regularly appear in BAAF's quarterly journal, *Adoption & Fostering*, which may be of interest to adoptive parents. For subscription details, contact BAAF or visit www.baaf.org.uk

Appendix

Principles of Video Interaction Guidance
(from H. Biemans)

Prepared by Nelleke Polderman, Basic Trust, Haarlem, The Netherlands
Translated By Arnoud Visser and Hilary Kennedy, Cupar, Fife, Scotland

 INITIATIVE or ACTION by the child
(words/verbal or behaviour, feeling, wish, thought)

 RECEPTION (confirmation) by the parent/educator

Step 1 | without words: | (friendly) intonation
turning to
eye contact
(friendly) expression
nodding
tone / sound of the
voice attuned

And:

with words:

- **CONFIRMATION OF RECEIPT** (repetition of what has been said / verbal initiative)

or

- **NAMING** (identifying) of behaviour, feelings, wishes, thoughts, intentions.

INITIATIVE of the educator / parent:

Step 2   give opinion
make yourself explicit
make a circle (divide turns)
study in depth
chatter
make a suggestion
name oppositions
positive prompting (offering a structure)
paying a compliment

Step 3   possibly after giving an opinion or making a suggestion:

Ask for a confirmation of receipt

or

Ask for a reaction to what has been said

INITIATIVE or (RE)ACTION of child, etc.